Sing, Spell Read&W

A Total Language Arts Curriculum
36 Steps to Independent Reading Ability

Assessment Book

17 Book End Assessments
for Phonetic Storybook Readers

3 Achievement Tests

Author
Sue Dickson

ISBN 1-56704-536-7
Printed in the United States of America
28 29 30 31 V056 19 18 17 16 15 14

Modern
Curriculum
Press

Pearson Learning Group

1-800-321-3106
www.pearsonlearning.com

Table of Contents
Book End Assessments

Assessment	Page(s)

Name

Date

Sing, Spell Read & Write ®

A Total Language Arts Curriculum
36 Steps to Independent Reading Ability

Book End Assessment for
Phonetic Storybook Reader 1

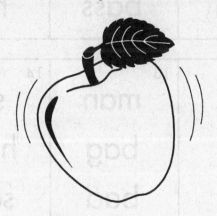

Student Assessment Record Summary RACEWAY STEP 6	Number Possible	Number Correct	Percentage of Mastery Score	
Word Recognition	20	____ x 5 =	_____ %	
Word Comprehension	20	____ x 5 =	_____ %	
Picture-Word Matching Fun................... (Word Comprehension)	20	____ x 5 =	_____ %	
Story Comprehension Matching Fun	10	____ x 10 =	_____ %	**Total Mastery Score:**
Missing Letter Fun............................. (Phonetic Analysis)	10	____ x 10 =	_____ %	
		Sum Of	_____ % ÷ 5 = ____ %	

Word Recognition and Word Comprehension

Name _____

1	2	3	4	5
cat	tag	pal	tax	cap
fan	Dad	at	wax	and
bat	hat	a	Nat	glad

6	7	8	9	10
Sam	van	pass	and	ham
map	mat	nap	bag	fan
tan	pan	bass	had	man

11	12	13	14	15
can	jam	man	sad	fast
wag	rag	bag	hand	last
fat	has	bad	sand	sat

16	17	18	19	20
ran	tap	mad	pat	Pam
sat	scat	ham	had	nap
Al	lap	jazz	slap	gas

Word Recognition [   ]   Word Comprehension [   ]

Number Correct   Number Correct

1 Storybook #1   Sing Spell Read & Write

Picture-Word Matching Fun
(Word Comprehension)

Name _____

 ă

1. van

2. hat

3. bag

4. fan

5. sad

6. gas

7. tan

8. map

9. cap

10. rat

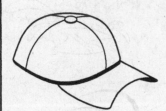

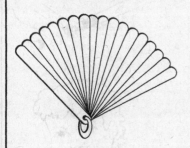

Go on

Picture-Word Matching Fun
(Word Comprehension)

Name _____

 ă

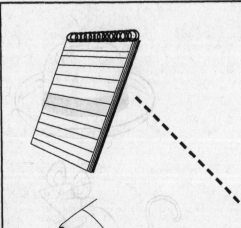

11. **sand**

12. **bass**

13. **pad**

14. **rap**

15. **lap**

16. **mad**

17. **tag**

18. **ham**

19. **bat**

20. **ran**

Picture-Word
Matching Fun

Number Correct

Sing Spell
Read & Write

Story Comprehension Matching Fun

Name _____

1. Dad has a bad cat.

2. Dad has a sad cat.

Sam!
Scat!

3. Dad has a pan
   and ham.

4. Dad has a fat cat.

5. Al has a fan and a hat.

Story Comprehension Matching Fun

Name _____

6. Nat had a nap.

7. Nat has a hat.

8. Al had jam.

9. A man had a bag.

10. A man has a tan.

Story Comprehension
Matching Fun

Number Correct

Missing Letter Fun
(Phonetic Analysis)

Name _____

1.

_ ag

2.

pa _

3.

an _

4.

_ at

5.

_ amp

6.

gl _ ss

7.

_ and

8.

_ ask

9.
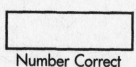
_ ack

10.
_ _ _ _ _ _ _ _ _ _
fla _

Missing Letter Fun

Number Correct

Copyright © Sue Dickson. Sing Spell Read & Write ® is a registered trademark of Pearson Education Inc.

Sing Spell Read & Write.

Storybook #1 6

Name

___ an   pa ___   ___ eg

gl ___ ss   ___ amp   at ___

___ ack   ask   and ___

Aa

Name _____

Date _____

A Total Language Arts Curriculum
36 Steps to Independent Reading Ability

Book End Assessment for
Phonetic Storybook Reader 2

Student Assessment Record Summary RACEWAY STEP 8	Number Possible	Number Correct	Percentage of Mastery Score	
Word Recognition	20	____	x 5 = _____ %	
Word Comprehension	20	____	x 5 = _____ %	
Picture-Word Matching Fun................. (Word Comprehension)	20	____	x 5 = _____ %	
Story Comprehension Matching Fun	10	____	x 10 = _____ %	**Total Mastery Score:**
Missing Letter Fun............................. (Phonetic Analysis)	10	____	x 10 = _____ %	
			Sum Of _____ % ÷ 5 = _____ %	

Word Recognition and Word Comprehension

Name _____

1 ten wet let	**2** tell red pet	**3** hen pen leg	**4** jet red yes	**5** mess less left
6 egg Ken mess	**7** sent peck pen	**8** help mend held	**9** bent held yell	**10** end bed red
11 fell tell yell	**12** bent nest next	**13** leg get gets	**14** sent help neck	**15** hen went eggs
16 less rest end	**17** Peg best fell	**18** mend ten bent	**19** wet bed yes	**20** nest fed well

Word Recognition [ ]
Number Correct

Word Comprehension [ ]
Number Correct

1 Storybook #2

Picture-Word Matching Fun
(Word Comprehension)

Name _____

◯ĕ

1. pet
2. beg
3. yell
4. fell
5. bent
6. mess
7. mend
8. well
9. sell
10. peck

Go on

Copyright © Sue Dickson, Sing Spell Read & Write ® is a registered trademark of Pearson Education Inc.

Picture-Word Matching Fun
(Word Comprehension)

Name _____

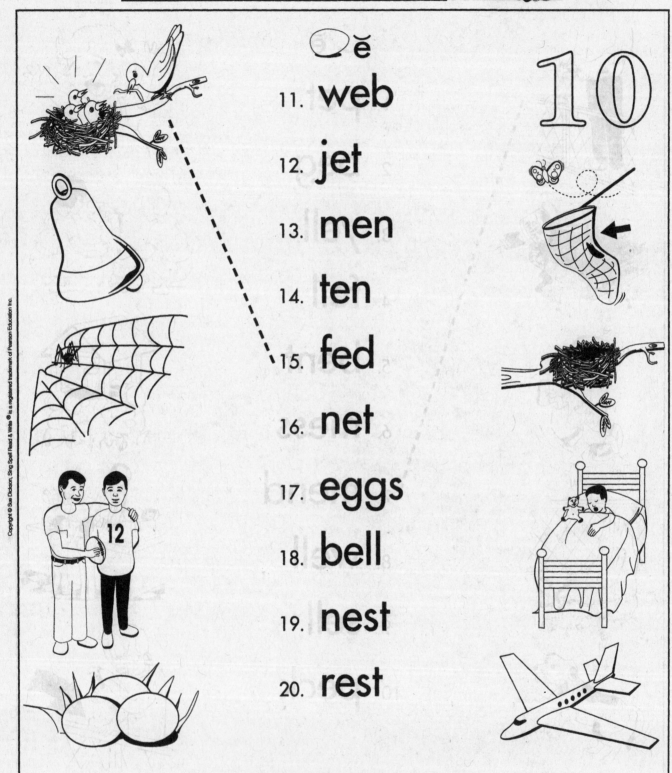

ĕ

11. web

12. jet

13. men

14. ten

15. fed

16. net

17. eggs

18. bell

19. nest

20. rest

10

Picture-Word Matching Fun

☐ Number Correct

Story Comprehension Matching Fun

Name _____

1. Sal has ten eggs!

2. Sal gets a red left leg!

3. Sal gets a red neck!

4. Sal gets fed.

5. Ken and Peg held Sal. Dad can help a wet hen.

Go on ➡

Copyright © Sue Dickson, Sing Spell Read & Write ® is a registered trademark of Pearson Education Inc.

Story Comprehension Matching Fun

Name _____

6. A neck has less red mess. Next, a left leg has less red mess.

7. Next, ten hen eggs have less red mess.

8. Sal went back and sat and sat.

9. Tap! Tap! Tap! Dad can mend the bent pen.

10. Well, at last Sal can rest.

Story Comprehension
Matching Fun

Number Correct

Missing Letter Fun
(Phonetic Analysis)

Name _____

1. __ed

2. ha__

3. ten__

4. __en

5. ma__

6. __gg

7. __eg

8. __esk

9. __an

10. pe__

Missing Letter Fun

Number Correct

Name

1. _ed

2. ha_

3. _ten

4. en_

5. ma_

6. _gg

7. _eg

8. esk_

9. _an

10. pe_

Missing
Letter Fun

Number Correct

Name _____

Date _____

A Total Language Arts Curriculum
36 Steps to Independent Reading Ability

Book End Assessment for
Phonetic Storybook Reader 3

Student Assessment Record Summary RACEWAY STEP 10	Number Possible	Number Correct	Percentage of Mastery Score	
Word Recognition	20	_____	x 5 = _____ %	
Word Comprehension	20	_____	x 5 = _____ %	
Picture-Word Matching Fun.......... (Word Comprehension)	20	_____	x 5 = _____ %	
Story Comprehension Matching Fun	10	_____	x10 = _____ %	**Total**
Missing Letter Fun.............................. (Phonetic Analysis)	10	_____	x10 = _____ %	**Mastery Score:**
			Sum Of _____ % ÷ 5 = _____ %	

Word Recognition and Word Comprehension

Name _____

1 if in sip	**2** yip sit miss	**3** it Biff lip	**4** six fill Sis	**5** pig Jim did
6 pin is big	**7** milk bib hill	**8** kick hit jig	**9** Ripp his lid	**10** him fit give
11 dig his did	**12** will bit quick	**13** mitt digs tin	**14** Jill Jim will	**15** Biff miss kiss
16 pig him big	**17** will milk fit	**18** whiz tip lift	**19** gift spill kiss	**20** it is in

Word Recognition [____]

Number Correct

Word Comprehension [____]

Number Correct

1 Storybook #3   Sing Spell Read & Write

Picture-Word Matching Fun
(Word Comprehension)

Name _____

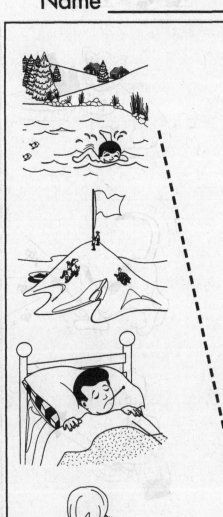

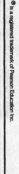

1. **tin can**

2. **kid**

3. **mix**

4. **ill**

5. **hill**

6. **kiss**

7. **mitt**

8. **milk**

9. **swim**

10. **gift**

Picture-Word Matching Fun
(Word Comprehension)

Name _____

11. pig

12. dig

13. hit

14. six

15. jig

16. yip

17. wig

18. lips

19. zip

20. bib

Picture-Word
Matching Fun

Number Correct

Story Comprehension Matching Fun

Name _____

1. Sis can sit and sip milk.

2. Jim has a mitt.

3. Biff has his milk
in a tin pan.

4. Sis has a pin.
Sis will give Biff a bib.

5. Jim is big.
Dad can tell Jim is big.

Go on →

Story Comprehension Matching Fun

Name _____

6. Dad will help Jim bat.

7. Jim can hit!
   Dad did help him.

*Teacher: To teach sequencing for numbers 8, 9, and 10, read (1) "what happened first" (2) "what happened next" (3) "what happened last".

8. Sis can have a
   big sand hill.

9. Sis can sit and dig
   in the sand.

10. Biff hid in the back.
    Biff can dig well.

1

2

3

Story Comprehension
Matching Fun

Number Correct

Missing Letter Fun
(Phonetic Analysis)

Name _____

1.

___ish

2.

fi___

3.

h___t

4.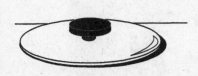

___id

5.

___ish

6.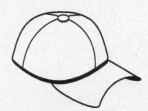

___ap

7.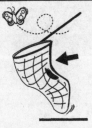

ne___

8.

___eb

9.

___ing

10.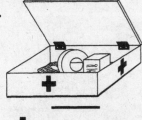

k___t

Missing Letter Fun [ ]

Number Correct

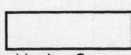

Phonetic Analysis

Name

ha_t

fi__

__ish

__ap

__ish

__id

__ing

__eb

__en

__k_t

Missing Letter Fun

Number Correct

Name   Date

Sing, Spell Read & Write ®

A Total Language Arts Curriculum
36 Steps to Independent Reading Ability

Book End Assessment for
Phonetic Storybook Reader 4

Student Assessment Record Summary RACEWAY STEP 12	Number Possible	Number Correct	Percentage of Mastery Score	
Word Recognition	20	____ x 5 =	_____ %	
Word Comprehension	20	____ x 5 =	_____ %	
Picture-Word Matching Fun (Word Comprehension)	20	____ x 5 =	_____ %	
Story Comprehension Matching Fun	10	____ x10 =	_____ %	**Total Mastery Score:**
Missing Letter Fun (Phonetic Analysis)	10	____ x10 =	_____ %	
		Sum Of	_____ % ÷ 5 = _____ %	

Word Recognition and Word Comprehension

Name _____

1	2	3	4	5
fox	rob	nod	hot	doll
top	box	hop	got	dog
spot	hog	dot	log	jog

6	7	8	9	10
Mom	not	hop	rob	ox
stop	pot	stop	hog	lot
hot	cot	log	from	Oz

11	12	13	14	15
Todd	on	log	not	lock
cot	lot	sock	pop	clock
tom-tom	top	dog	odd	rock

16	17	18	19	20
odd	pop	rock	fox	sock
on	spot	not	top	blocks
doll	stop	lock	box	pot

Word Recognition [ ]

Word Comprehension [ ]

Number Correct

Number Correct

1 Storybook #4

Sing-Spell Read&Write.

Picture-Word Matching Fun
(Word Comprehension)

Name _____

 ŏ

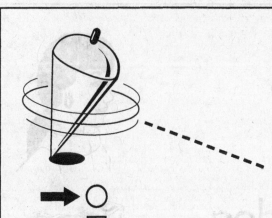

1. hog

2. top

3. cob

4. rob

5. ox

6. dot

7. hop

8. fox

9. box

10. sob

Picture-Word Matching Fun
(Word Comprehension)

Name _____

ŏ

11. mop

12. cot

13. hot dog

14. rod

15. jog

16. mom

17. tom-tom

18. doll

19. sock

20. blocks

Picture-Word
Matching Fun

Number Correct

Story Comprehension Matching Fun

Name _____

1. Pep got on his cot.
   At last, Pep can rest.

2. Todd had a bat.
   Todd had a lock.

3. Todd had a tom-tom.

4. Jill has a doll.
   Jill's doll is Kim.

Story Comprehension Matching Fun

Name _____

 RACEWAY STEP **12** ŏ

5. Jill set Kim on the doll bed.

6. Pep hid Kim in the big pot.

7. Jill went to get Kim. Kim was not in bed.

> *Teacher: To teach sequencing for numbers 8, 9, and 10, read (1) "what happened first" (2) "what happened next" (3) "what happened last".

8. Pep got the doll from the pot.

1

9. Jill ran to Todd. Kim is not in the bed.

2

10. Todd did not have Kim.

3

Copyright © Sue Dickson, Sing Spell Read & Write ® is a registered trademark of Pearson Education Inc.

5 Storybook #4   Story Comprehension Matching Fun ⬚ Number Correct

Missing Letter Fun
(Phonetic Analysis)

Name _____

1.

__ ot

2.

do __

3.

m __ tt

4.

__ ocks

5.

__ est

6.

__ og

7.

p __ p

8.

__ ag

9.

si __

10.

__ am

Missing
Letter Fun

Number Correct

Name _____

1. t o ___
2. ___ o b
3. m ___ tt
4. ___ o cks
5. ___ est
6. ___ o g
7. b ___ b
8. ___ o g
9. si ___
10. ___ am

Name _____

Date _____

Sing,Spell Read&Write ®

A Total Language Arts Curriculum
36 Steps to Independent Reading Ability

Book End Assessment for
Phonetic Storybook Reader 5

Student Assessment Record Summary RACEWAY STEP 14	Number Possible	Number Correct	Percentage of Mastery Score	
Word Recognition	20	____ x 5 =	_____ %	
Word Comprehension	20	____ x 5 =	_____ %	
Picture-Word Matching Fun................. (Word Comprehension)	20	____ x 5 =	_____ %	
Story Comprehension Matching Fun	10	____ x 10 =	_____ %	**Total**
Missing Letter Fun............................. (Phonetic Analysis)	10	____ x 10 =	_____ %	**Mastery Score:**
		Sum Of	_____ % ÷ 5 =	_____ %

Word Recognition and Word Comprehension

Name _____

1 sun / rub / mud	**2** bug / nut / tub	**3** bus / Gus / cup	**4** hum / mug / but	**5** fun / dug / cut
6 up / us / but	**7** duck / bun / fuss	**8** cup / dump / tug	**9** rug / buzz / pup	**10** run / bud / gulp
11 fuzz / drum / snug	**12** dug / bug / bun	**13** hut / stuck / gum	**14** fun / mud / nut	**15** cups / dust / us
16 truck / umbrella / jump	**17** dull / tub / cut	**18** hum / jump / snug	**19** must / puff / duck	**20** puff / fuss / fuzz

Word Recognition [   ]   Word Comprehension [   ]

Number Correct   Number Correct

1 Storybook #5   Sing-Spell Read&Write

Picture-Word Matching Fun
(Word Comprehension)

Name _____

 ŭ

1. **gum**

2. **bug**

3. **rug**

4. **mug**

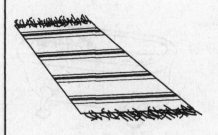

5. **nut**

6. **bun**

7. **cup**

8. **bus**

9. **hum**

10. **bud**

Copyright © Sue Dickson, Sing Spell Read & Write ® is a registered trademark of Pearson Education Inc.

Go on ⟶

Picture-Word Matching Fun
(Word Comprehension)

Name _____

 ŭ

11. **sun**

12. **mud**

13. **pup**

14. **drum**

15. **duck**

16. **truck**

17. **dust**

18. **cut**

19. **tub**

20. **jump**

Picture-Word
Matching Fun

Number Correct

3 Storybook #5

Story Comprehension Matching Fun

Name _____

1. Gus has fun in gum,
   but Gus can get stuck!

2. Gus and Max have fun
   in a cup.

3. Tom must run fast
   to the bus.

4. Gus has a truck.
   Gus has fun.

Story Comprehension Matching Fun

Name _____

5. Gus has a drum.
   Gus has jazz.

6. Gus and Max can hum
   and hum.

7. Tom has a pup.

*Teacher: To teach sequencing for numbers 8, 9, and 10, read (1) "what happened first" (2) "what happened next" (3) "what happened last".

8. Rub-a-dub-dub!
   Dad rubs a bug in the tub.

                                                    1

9. Gus is in bed.
   Gus is glad.

                                                    2

                                                    3

10. Dad will fill the tub.

Sing Spell Read & Write.

Story Comprehension
Matching Fun

Number Correct

Missing Letter Fun
(Phonetic Analysis)

Name _____

1.

__ub

2.

__og

3.

__od

4.

__ift

5.

__ug

6.

w__g

7.

__ut

8.

fo__

9.

hu__

10.

__awn

Missing
Letter Fun

Number Correct

Missing Letter Fun

(Phonetic Answers)

Name _____

Name _____

Date _____

Sing, Spell Read&Write ®

A Total Language Arts Curriculum
36 Steps to Independent Reading Ability

Book End Assessment for
Phonetic Storybook Reader 6

PICK-UP TRUCK

Student Assessment Record Summary RACEWAY STEP 15	Number Possible	Number Correct	Percentage of Mastery Score	
Word Recognition	20	_____	x 5 = _____ %	
Word Comprehension	20	_____	x 5 = _____ %	
Sentence Comprehension...................	20	_____	x 5 = _____ %	**Total Mastery Score:**
Story Comprehension	5	_____	x 20 = _____ %	
		Sum Of	_____ % ÷ 4 = _____ %	

Word Recognition and Word Comprehension

Name _____

1	2	3	4	5
lump	stick	sand	lift	dust
lamp	snack	send	list	dump
land	spend	sock	limp	dots

6	7	8	9	10
just	melt	test	Rick	hunt
jump	mend	tack	duck	bump
Jack	milk	tent	desk	hand

11	12	13	14	15
grand	best	truck	belt	fact
gulp	bend	clock	block	fast
gift	band	stick	bulb	fist

16	17	18	19	20
sock	must	pill	damp	from
sick	mask	pick	dump	frog
sift	mend	pond	duck	fond

Word Recognition [ ]

Number Correct

Word Comprehension [ ]

Number Correct

1 Storybook #6   Sing Spell Read & Write.

Sentence Comprehension

Name _____

RACEWAY STEP **15** more ă ĕ ĭ ŏ ŭ

1. The man hit his fist on the rug.

A ○   B ○   C ○   D ○

A

2. The man has a rust rug.

A ○   B ○   C ○   D ○

B

3. Mom went to get a rug.

A ○   B ○   C ○   D ○

C

Yes, I have a rust rug.

4. Mom had to ask, "Will the rug cost a lot?"

A ○   B ○   C ○   D ○

D

Copyright © Sue Dickson. Sing Spell Read & Write ® is a registered trademark of Pearson Education Inc.

Sing Spell Read & Write   Storybook #6 **2**

Sentence Comprehension

Name _____

5. Ted gets gas in his truck.

A ○   B ○   C ○   D ○

6. The red truck went up the hill.

A ○   B ○   C ○   D ○

7. It went past a frog.

A ○   B ○   C ○   D ○

8. It went past a mat.

A ○   B ○   C ○   D ○

A
B   GAS $1.19 +TAX
C   WELCOME
D   flap flap

Sing Spell Read & Write.

Sentence Comprehension

Name _____

9. Dad will fix the desk on the rug.

A ○   B ○   C ○   D ○

A

10. Mom will fix the lamp on the rug.

A ○   B ○   C ○   D ○

B

11. Dad can lift the rug. Mom will help.

A ○   B ○   C ○   D ○

C

12. Dad will tack the rug.

A ○   B ○   C ○   D ○

D

Copyright © Sue Dickson. Sing Spell Read & Write ® is a registered trademark of Pearson Education Inc.

Sentence Comprehension

13. Bill went to camp.

    A   B   C   D
    ○   ○   ○   ○

A

14. "Let's jump back
    in the pond," said Bill.

    A   B   C   D
    ○   ○   ○   ○

B

WELCOME TO WEST CAMP

15. Bill can kick and swim.

    A   B   C   D
    ○   ○   ○   ○

C

16. Bill has a pal.

    A   B   C   D
    ○   ○   ○   ○

D

Sing Spell Read & Write

Sentence Comprehension

Name _____

17. Jill had a spill. A ○　B ○　C ○　D ○	A
18. Jill has a red leg. A ○　B ○　C ○　D ○	B
19. Mom will help Jill. A ○　B ○　C ○　D ○	C
20. Jill ran fast. A ○　B ○　C ○　D ○	D

Story Comprehension

Rick has a band.
Don has a drum.
Bob can strum.
Jill can hum.
Rick will tap.
"A band is a lot of fun," said Rick.

1. _____ had a band.

   Don   Jill   Rick   Bob
   ○   ○   ○   ○

2. Rick is _____.

   glad   sad   mad   bad
   ○   ○   ○   ○

3. How many are in the band?

   5   4   3   30
   ○   ○   ○   ○

4. This story is about a _____.

   class   band   picnic   hat
   ○   ○   ○   ○

5. Jill can _____.

   sing   clap   tap   hum
   ○   ○   ○   ○

Story Comprehension

Number Correct

Name _____   **Date** _____

A Total Language Arts Curriculum
36 Steps to Independent Reading Ability

Book End Assessment for
Phonetic Storybook Reader 7

Student Assessment Record Summary RACEWAY STEPS 19 - 20	Number Possible	Number Correct	Percentage of Mastery Score	
Word Recognition	20	_____ × 5 =	_____ %	
Word Comprehension	20	_____ × 5 =	_____ %	
Sentence Comprehension	25	_____ × 4 =	_____ %	**Total**
Story Comprehension.........................	10	_____ ×10 =	_____ %	**Mastery Score:**
		Sum Of _____ % ÷ 4 =	_____ %	

Word Recognition and Word Comprehension

Name _____

1	2	3	4	5
beach	cream	leaf	team	spear
beak	clear	leap	tear	speak
beast	gear	lean	tea	stream

6	7	8	9	10
seat	beam	feel	sheet	seed
seal	bead	feed	street	seek
seam	beak	feet	sheep	seen

11	12	13	14	15
sweep	tried	screen	weep	pie
sweet	tree	green	wheel	peep
sheet	three	queen	wheat	peak

16	17	18	19	20
cheer	snail	nail	gain	faith
creep	nail	mail	paint	fail
coat	sail	maid	pain	hail

Word Recognition ⬜
Number Correct

Word Comprehension ⬜
Number Correct

1 Storybook #7   Sing Spell Read&Write®

Sentence Comprehension

Name _____

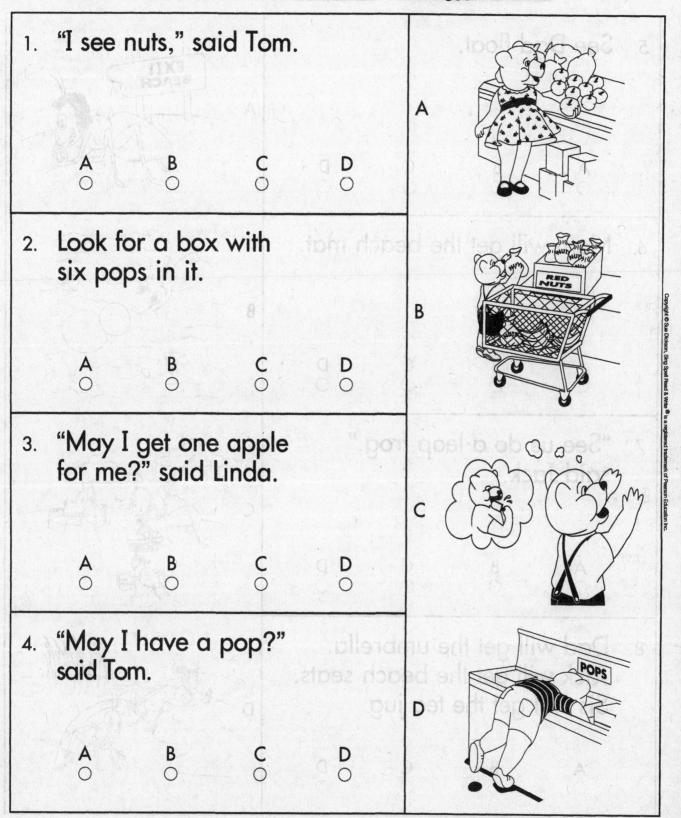

1. "I see nuts," said Tom.

   A ◯   B ◯   C ◯   D ◯

2. Look for a box with six pops in it.

   A ◯   B ◯   C ◯   D ◯

3. "May I get one apple for me?" said Linda.

   A ◯   B ◯   C ◯   D ◯

4. "May I have a pop?" said Tom.

   A ◯   B ◯   C ◯   D ◯

A

B

C

D

Sentence Comprehension

Name _____

5. See Dad float.

   A   B   C   D
   ○   ○   ○   ○

6. Mom will get the beach mat.

   A   B   C   D
   ○   ○   ○   ○

7. "See us do a leap frog,"
said Jack.

   A   B   C   D
   ○   ○   ○   ○

8. Dad will get the umbrella.
Jack will get the beach seats.
Sis will get the tea jug.

   A   B   C   D
   ○   ○   ○   ○

A   EXIT BEACH

B

C

D

Sing Spell Read & Write

Sentence Comprehension

Name _____

9. "We have peaches and cream," Mom said.

   A ○   B ○   C ○   D ○

 A

10. "I have lean meat and green beans for us," said Mom.

    A ○   B ○   C ○   D ○

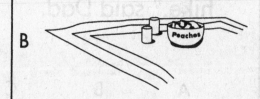 B

11. "I will set up the beach umbrella," said Dad.

    A ○   B ○   C ○   D ○

 C

12. "We will go to the beach," said Mom.

    A ○   B ○   C ○   D ○

 D

Sentence Comprehension

Name _____

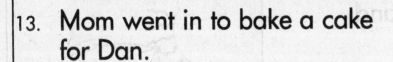

13. Mom went in to bake a cake for Dan.

    A   B   C   D
    ○   ○   ○   ○

A

14. "Yes, you may go on a bike hike," said Dad.

    A   B   C   D
    ○   ○   ○   ○

B

15. "We will see you at six o'clock," said Jake and Mike.

    A   B   C   D
    ○   ○   ○   ○

C

16. "Here we go!" said Jake and Mike.

    A   B   C   D
    ○   ○   ○   ○

D

Sing, Spell, Read & Write.

Sentence Comprehension

Name _____

17. "We must take the trail map," said Pat.

   A   B   C   D
   ○   ○   ○   ○

A — I will take the trail map.

18. Up the trail they went.

   A   B   C   D
   ○   ○   ○   ○

B

19. "Here is a Band-Aid from my kit. This will keep it clean," said Dave.

   A   B   C   D
   ○   ○   ○   ○

C

20. "Be back here by five o'clock," said Mom.
"Fine. That will give us lots of time," said Meg.

   A   B   C   D
   ○   ○   ○   ○

D

Sentence Comprehension

RACEWAY STEP **20** two vowels, silent ø, c = s

21. She liked to clean the rug. She got it nice and clean.

A ○   B ○   C ○   D ○   E ○

A

22. Mom's face went into a big smile.

A ○   B ○   C ○   D ○   E ○

B

23. "Mom likes this lace one," said Alice. "Help me place it on the table, Grace."

A ○   B ○   C ○   D ○   E ○

C

24. "You can go to buy the ice cream. Just tell me the price when you get back," said Mom.

A ○   B ○   C ○   D ○   E ○

D

25. "Mmm," said Grace. "That spice cake smells nice, Mom."

A ○   B ○   C ○   D ○   E ○

E

Sentence Comprehension

Number Correct

Story Comprehension

Name _____

> "We will go to the Snack Hut," said Mom. "We will buy some snacks. Come with me."
>
> "Here we come," said Jim and Tom.
>
> "Yes," said Linda. "We like snacks. We will come with you, Mom."
>
> "We do not have very many apples," said Jim. "We like apples. May we buy some?
>
> "Yes, I will buy some apples for you," said Mom.

1. Why will Mom go to the Snack Hut?

   ○ to see Jim, Tom and Linda

   ○ to buy snacks

   ○ to sing a song

   ○ to buy wax

Go on ➡

Story Comprehension

RACEWAY STEP **19** Sight words

2. _____ went to the Snack Hut.

   - ○ Mom, Dan, Tim and Linda
   - ○ Bill, Dad, Jack and Pam
   - ○ Peg, Pam, Tom and Dick
   - ○ Mom, Jim, Tom and Linda

3. Can Mom buy a dress at the Snack Hut?

   Yes   No
   ○   ○

4. Jim, Tom and Linda are _____.

   sad   mad   bad   glad
   ○   ○   ○   ○

5. This is about _____.

   - ○ a trip to camp
   - ○ a trip to the Snack Hut
   - ○ two apples
   - ○ Mom has ham

Go on →

Sing Spell Read & Write

Story Comprehension

Look back if you need help.

Joe came home. He held a nest in his hand.

"Mom, Mom, see what I have!" he said.

"That is nice, Joe," said Mom, "but you must place it back in the tree at once."

"Yes, Mom," said Joe. "A nest is best in a tree. The bird can come back to the nest if it is in the tree."

Joe was back fast. "Let me help you too, Mom," he said. "What can I do?"

"You are nice, Joe," said Mom. "Yes, I can use your help."

6. Joe had a _____ in his hand.

dog ○   cat ○   nest ○   cap ○

7. When must Joe place the nest back in the tree?

five o'clock ○   now ○   love ○   six o'clock ○

Go on

Story Comprehension

Look back if you need help.

RACEWAY STEP **20** two vowels, silent ø, c = s

8. Why did Joe place the nest in the tree?

   ○ So the bird can come back

   ○ It was not his

   ○ Sis said to place it in the tree

   ⊙ To look at it

9. Could this story happen?

   Yes   No

   ○   ○

10. What did Joe ask Mom?

    ○ May I go?

    ○ Will Dave come?

    ○ What can I do?

    ○ What will we eat?

Sing Spell Read & Write

Story Comprehension

Number Correct

Name   Date

Book End Assessment for
Phonetic Storybook Reader 8

Student Assessment Record Summary RACEWAY STEP 21	Number Possible	Number Correct	Percentage of Mastery Score	
Word Recognition	20	___ x 5 =	_____ %	
Word Comprehension	20	___ x 5 =	_____ %	
Sentence Comprehension	25	___ x 4 =	_____ %	**Total Mastery Score:**
Story Comprehension	10	___ x10 =	_____ %	
		Sum Of	_____ % ÷ 4 =	_____ %

Word Recognition and Word Comprehension

Name _____

1	2	3	4	5
pay	bay	way	clay	say
stay	day	jay	play	ray
play	hay	pay	lay	may

6	7	8	9	10
hay	stay	play	shy	pay
bay	ray	clay	sky	spy
say	tray	stay	sly	cry

11	12	13	14	15
fly	by	try	sly	sky
fry	my	dry	why	shy
try	why	fry	fly	why

16	17	18	19	20
germ	hinge	page	bulge	huge
gem	huge	age	giant	germ
giant	bulge	germ	hinge	page

Word Recognition ☐   Word Comprehension ☐

Number Correct   Number Correct

Sentence Comprehension

Name _____

1. It is a boat race with one, two, three, four, five, six, seven, eight, nine, ten boats!

   A ○ B ○ C ○ D ○ E ○

   A

2. The red boat wins the race!

   A ○ B ○ C ○ D ○ E ○

   B

3. The pink boat is tenth!

   A ○ B ○ C ○ D ○ E ○

   C

4. A man limped up the road.

   A ○ B ○ C ○ D ○ E ○

   D

5. A lady is mailing a letter.

   A ○ B ○ C ○ D ○ E ○

   E

Sentence Comprehension

RACEWAY STEP **21** | āy, y=ī, g=j, y=e
Suffixes: er, ed, ing

6. I will make a clay blue jay.

A ○   B ○   C ○   D ○   E ○

A

7. Good-by, blue jay; have a nice day!

A ○   B ○   C ○   D ○   E ○

B

Jay!
Jay

8. Ray went to swim in the bay.

A ○   B ○   C ○   D ○   E ○

C

CLAY BLUE GRAY WHITE MADE USA

9. In this nest my eggs I lay!

A ○   B ○   C ○   D ○   E ○

D

CLAY

10. She will not lay eggs on the hay.

A ○   B ○   C ○   D ○   E ○

E

Sing Spell Read & Write

Sentence Comprehension

11. **A little fly came by.**

A ○ B ○ C ○ D ○ E ○

A

12. **You just pry up the sh from shy.**

A ○ B ○ C ○ D ○ E ○

B

13. **I see a flag waving on top of the hill.**

A ○ B ○ C ○ D ○ E ○

C

14. **This made the huge giant bulge with pride!**

A ○ B ○ C ○ D ○ E ○

D

15. **A huge giant was crying and crying.**

A ○ B ○ C ○ D ○ E ○

E

Sentence Comprehension

RACEWAY STEP **21**

āy, y=ī, g=j, y=e
Suffixes: er, ed, ing

16. **Sally is fussy!**

    A   B   C   D   E
    ○   ○   ○   ○   ○

    A

17. **Billy and Gary came up the street.**

    A   B   C   D   E
    ○   ○   ○   ○   ○

    B

18. **Freddy had his kite in his hand.**

    A   B   C   D   E
    ○   ○   ○   ○   ○

    C

19. **Lucy likes to baby-sit Sally.**

    A   B   C   D   E
    ○   ○   ○   ○   ○

    D

20. **"Here, Sally, have some jellybeans," said Lucy.**

    A   B   C   D   E
    ○   ○   ○   ○   ○

    E

Sing Spell Read & Write.

Sentence Comprehension

Name _____

21. A kid played his flute and a drummer was drumming his drum.

    A ○   B ○   C ○   D ○   E ○

22. "I see a man painting an ad!" yelled Patty.

    A ○   B ○   C ○   D ○   E ○

23. A batter has batted the ball and is running to the base.

    A ○   B ○   C ○   D ○   E ○

24. Patty and Harry just sat and rested.

    A ○   B ○   C ○   D ○   E ○

25. Mommy said, "I just baked and iced a cake."

    A ○   B ○   C ○   D ○   E ○

Sentence Comprehension

Number Correct

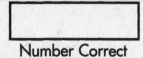

Storybook #8 **6**

Story Comprehension

RACEWAY STEP **21**
āy, y=ī, g=j, y=e
Suffixes: er, ed, ing

> Lucy is nine. She likes to baby-sit. Sally is pretty and she is happy.
>
> "Here, Sally, have some jellybeans," said Lucy. "Red, yellow, pink and green jellybeans."
>
> "I like candy," said Sally, "and I love jellybeans!"

1. Lucy is _____.

   two   three   nine   one
   ○   ○   ○   ○

2. What is Lucy doing?
   - ○ She is playing.
   - ○ She is baby-sitting.
   - ○ She is sleeping.
   - ○ She is crying.

3. Who is Lucy baby-sitting?
   Freddy   Billy   Sue   Sally
   ○   ○   ○   ○

4. Lucy gave Sally some _____.
   apples   jellybeans   a kite   a dog
   ○   ○   ○   ○

Go on →

Sing Spell Read & Write

Story Comprehension

Look back if you need help.

5. Did Sally like the jellybeans?

   Yes   No
   ○   ○

It was a hot day! Patty and Harry just sat and rested. Patty licked a pop. Harry licked a pop, too! The pops melted fast!

Daddy came home. He said, "We have not camped yet this summer. Your Mommy and I will take you camping."

6. What did Patty and Harry do?

   ○ sat and rested

   ○ sang and played

   ○ had a nap

   ○ cry

7. Why did the pops melt?

   ○ Harry and Patty would not eat them.

   ○ Pops melt when it is hot.

   ○ Harry sat on them.

   ○ Patty had them in a box.

Go on

Story Comprehension

Look back if you need help.

8. Do Patty and Harry like to camp?

   Yes   No

   ○   ○

9. What time of year was it?

   spring   winter   summer   fall

   ○   ○   ○   ○

10. Which word will <u>not</u> fit?

    Mommy   Daddy   rain   Patty

    ○   ○   ○   ○

   Sing Spell Read & Write   Story Comprehension

Number Correct

Name _____

Date _____

Sing, Spell Read & Write ®

A Total Language Arts Curriculum
36 Steps to Independent Reading Ability

Book End Assessment for
Phonetic Storybook Reader 9

Student Assessment Record Summary RACEWAY STEP 22	Number Possible	Number Correct	Percentage of Mastery Score	
Word Recognition	20	____	x 5 = ____ %	
Word Comprehension	20	____	x 5 = ____ %	
Sentence Comprehension	20	____	x 5 = ____ %	**Total**
				Mastery
Story Comprehension	10	____	x 10 = ____ %	**Score:**
		Sum Of	____ % ÷ 4 = ____ %	

Word Recognition and Word Comprehension

1	2	3	4	5
fort	sort	horn	storm	core
torn	cord	form	store	corn
fork	sore	born	short	for

6	7	8	9	10
stork	north	torch	port	dash
cord	thorn	scorch	sport	hash
pork	short	order	sort	mash

11	12	13	14	15
shore	rush	shin	wish	sheet
shine	crush	ship	sash	sheep
shave	cash	fish	rash	shorts

16	17	18	19	20
shut	mush	shoot	short	shell
shoe	crash	shot	shade	she
hush	plush	shop	shake	shelf

Word Recognition [   ]   Word Comprehension [   ]

Number Correct   Number Correct

Sentence Comprehension

Name _____

1. "I see a box," yelled Kate. "It has a big stork on it." "Here is a big apple box," said Kevin. He nearly fell in it!

    A ○   B ○   C ○   D ○

A

2. "We will sort the boxes. We will not get a wet one or a torn one," said Kevin.

    A ○   B ○   C ○   D ○

B

3. "It was a big job to make a hot rod," said Mom. "Here is a glass of punch and a chunk of chocolate to munch."

    A ○   B ○   C ○   D ○

C

4. "No, I just hit my shin and my shorts got ripped," said Sheldon. "I wish I had not gone so fast!"

    A ○   B ○   C ○   D ○

D

Sentence Comprehension

Name _____

5. "I will name my hot rod Red Flash. I will be a champ in my Red Flash," said Gus.

   A   B   C   D
   ○   ○   ○   ○

A

6. "I would like to try on the red shorts, the green ones, the gray ones and the yellow shirt," said Jenny.

   A   B   C   D
   ○   ○   ○   ○

B

7. Just then some children shot a rocket into the sky.

   A   B   C   D
   ○   ○   ○   ○

C

8. "Let's turn onto North Street," said Curly.

   A   B   C   D
   ○   ○   ○   ○

D

Sing Spell Read & Write.

Sentence Comprehension

Name _____

9. On his way he met a big dog. The big dog had brown and white fur. His tail had a big curl in it.

   A ○   B ○   C ○   D ○

A

10. "Wait, wait," said the clerk. She was very stern.

    A ○   B ○   C ○   D ○

B

11. "My legs will be sore before we get to North Street," said Kevin.

    A ○   B ○   C ○   D ○

C

12. See Kevin and Kate's fort! What fun they will have!

    A ○   B ○   C ○   D ○

D

Sentence Comprehension

Name _____

13. "Yes, you may go to the store," said Mom. "You can pick up my order. It is on this list."

    A ○ B ○ C ○ D ○

A

14. Each day the children eat lunch in the Lunch Hut. They sit on a bench. Not one inch of the bench is left to sit on!

    A ○ B ○ C ○ D ○

B

15. "Third, we will turn it over and lift up the pail," said Shirley.

    A ○ B ○ C ○ D ○

C

16. "Look," said Bert. "I see a bird. Did you hear it chirp up in our fir tree? He is asking if our cake is real."

    A ○ B ○ C ○ D ○

D

Sing Spell Read & Write.

Sentence Comprehension

Name _____

17. After rest time, the children go to the beach. They chase each other across the sand to the lake.

    A   B   C   D
    ○   ○   ○   ○

18. Kevin said, "What can we do for fun?"
    "We can make a fort for fun," said Kate.

    A   B   C   D
    ○   ○   ○   ○

19. Shirley said, "Here, Bert. You may make the swirls on top. Use the curved stick to make swirls."

    A   B   C   D
    ○   ○   ○   ○

20. "What did you do?" asked his Mom. "I fell off my bike," said Sheldon. "My bike hit a stone and I flipped!"

    A   B   C   D
    ○   ○   ○   ○

A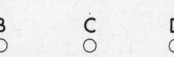

B

C

D

Sentence Comprehension

Number Correct

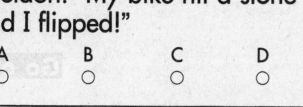

Story Comprehension

Name _____

"I would like to make a hot rod," said Gus.
"I would like to race it in the Hot Rod Race."
   "Fine," said Dad. "I will help you make it."
   Each day Dad and Gus did more.
   Dad said, "We need a chain. You can reach it, Gus."
   "Yes, Dad," said Gus. "Will you need a torch, too?"
   "No," said Dad. "That will scorch it. A torch is just for metal."

1. What would Gus like to make?

   a hot rod   a box   a can   a hot dog
      ○   ○   ○   ○

2. Will Gus race his hot rod in the Hot Rod Race?
      Yes   No
       ○   ○

3. Did Gus and Dad make the hot rod in one day?
      Yes   No
       ○   ○

Go on ➡

Story Comprehension

Look back if you need help.

4. The torch is used for _____.

    glass   wax   paper   metal

    ○   ○   ○   ○

5. Why did Dad <u>not</u> use the torch?

    ○   It was too big.

    ○   It was bent.

    ○   It would scorch.

    ○   He did not have it.

"Mommy! The term is over! I'm a third grader now! yelled Jenny. "May we go to the seashore?" she asked.

"Yes, we will go next Thursday," said Mom. "Dad can come with us then."

"Yippee!" cried Jenny. "I love the seashore, but I need some bigger shorts and shirts."

"Fine," said Mom. "Let's go to the shop on Third Street."

Jenny and her mom went to the store to shop.

Go on ➡

Story Comprehension

Look back if you need help.

"I need a skirt," said Mom.
"I would like shorts and a shirt," said Jenny.
"We need a clerk," said Mom. "A clerk can help us."

6. What grade is Jenny going to be in?

first	second	third	fourth
○	○	○	○

7. Why will they wait until next Thursday to go to the seashore?

○ The term was not over.

○ So Dad can go with them.

○ It will rain.

○ Mom cannot go today.

8. Jenny was a _____ last term.

○ second grader

○ first grader

○ fourth grader

○ boy

Go on ➡

Story Comprehension

Look back if you need help.

9. Jenny will find _____ in the shop on Third Street.

   ○ beds

   ○ shorts and shirts

   ○ bike

   ○ candy

10. Jenny will feel _____ when she gets to the seashore.

| sad | mad | fussy | happy |
| ○ | ○ | ○ | ○ |

Story Comprehension [   ]

Number Correct

Sing Spell Read & Write.   Storybook #9 **10**

Name _____

Date _____

Sing, Spell Read & Write ®

A Total Language Arts Curriculum
36 Steps to Independent Reading Ability

Book End Assessment for
Phonetic Storybook Reader 10

Student Assessment Record Summary RACEWAY STEP 23	Number Possible	Number Correct	Percentage of Mastery Score	
Word Recognition	20	_____ x 5 =	_____ %	
Word Comprehension	20	_____ x 5 =	_____ %	
Sentence Comprehension....................	20	_____ x 5 =	_____ %	**Total**
				Mastery
Story Comprehension	10	_____ x10 =	_____ %	**Score:**
		Sum Of	_____ % ÷ 4 =	_____ %

Word Recognition and Word Comprehension

Name _____

1	2	3	4	5
the	them	cloth	think	that
them	there	moth	thing	their
thick	three	broth	this	thank

6	7	8	9	10
with	match	thin	these	latch
stitch	catch	thank	those	pitch
Smith	patch	thick	both	sketch

11	12	13	14	15
latch	crutch	moth	their	Smith
ditch	stretch	with	there	both
itch	scratch	them	three	cloth

16	17	18	19	20
patch	three	those	they	with
pitch	crutch	ditch	then	itch
itch	catch	stretch	this	thin

Word Recognition [   ]

Number Correct

Word Comprehension [   ]

Number Correct

1 Storybook #10   Sing·Spell Read&Write.

Sentence Comprehension

Name _____

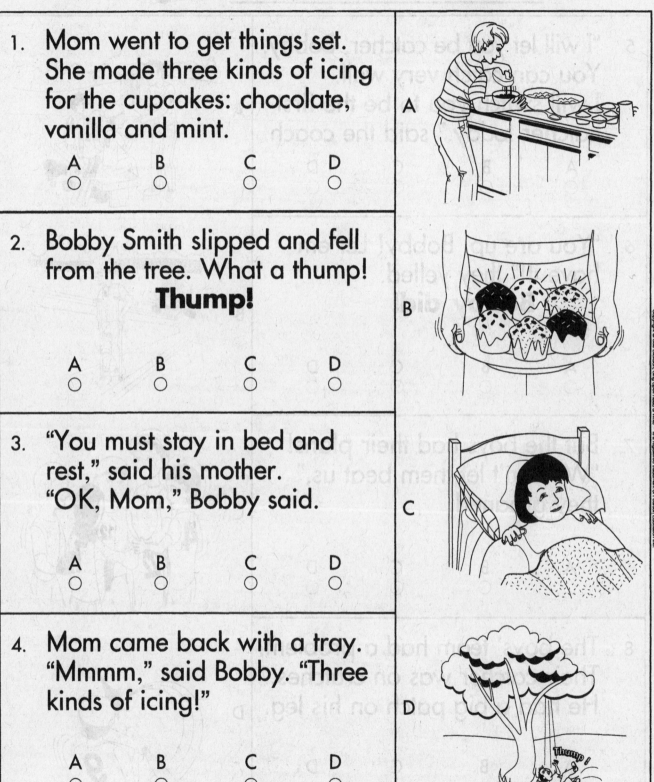

1. Mom went to get things set. She made three kinds of icing for the cupcakes: chocolate, vanilla and mint.

   A   B   C   D
   ○   ○   ○   ○

2. Bobby Smith slipped and fell from the tree. What a thump! **Thump!**

   A   B   C   D
   ○   ○   ○   ○

3. "You must stay in bed and rest," said his mother. "OK, Mom," Bobby said.

   A   B   C   D
   ○   ○   ○   ○

4. Mom came back with a tray. "Mmmm," said Bobby. "Three kinds of icing!"

   A   B   C   D
   ○   ○   ○   ○

Sentence Comprehension

Name _____

5. "I will let you be catcher, Bobby.
You can catch very well.
I will switch you to be the first
catcher today," said the coach.

A B C D
○ ○ ○ ○

A

6. "You are up, Bobby! Let 'em
have it!" they yelled.
Bobby did!

A B C D
○ ○ ○ ○

B

7. But the boys had their plans!
"We can't let them beat us,"
they groaned.

A B C D
○ ○ ○ ○

C

8. The boys' team had a problem.
Their catcher was on crutches.
He had a big patch on his leg.

A B C D
○ ○ ○ ○

D

Sing Spell Read & Write.

Sentence Comprehension

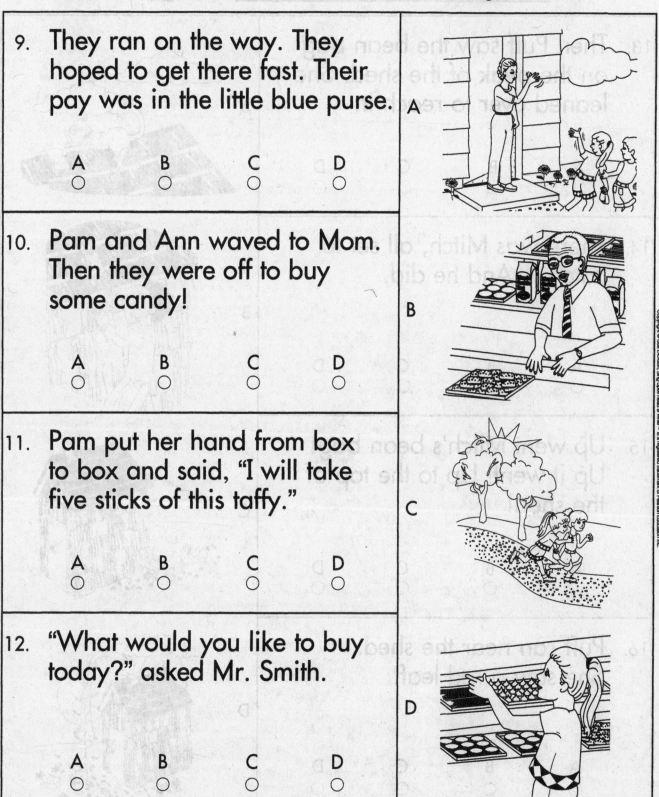

9. They ran on the way. They hoped to get there fast. Their pay was in the little blue purse.

    A   B   C   D
    ○   ○   ○   ○

10. Pam and Ann waved to Mom. Then they were off to buy some candy!

    A   B   C   D
    ○   ○   ○   ○

11. Pam put her hand from box to box and said, "I will take five sticks of this taffy."

    A   B   C   D
    ○   ○   ○   ○

12. "What would you like to buy today?" asked Mr. Smith.

    A   B   C   D
    ○   ○   ○   ○

Copyright © Sue Dickson, Sing Spell Read & Write ® is a registered trademark of Pearson Education Inc.

Sentence Comprehension

Name _____

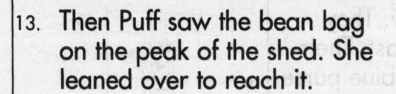

RACEWAY STEP **23** th, tch

13. Then Puff saw the bean bag on the peak of the shed. She leaned over to reach it.

A ○   B ○   C ○   D ○

A

14. There was Mitch, all set to catch it. And he did.

A ○   B ○   C ○   D ○

B

15. Up went Mitch's bean bag! Up it went! Up to the top of the shed!

A ○   B ○   C ○   D ○

C

16. Puff ran near the shed. She saw a red leaf.

A ○   B ○   C ○   D ○

D

Sing Spell Read & Write.

Sentence Comprehension

Name _____

17. With the ABC code you can read anything you want. There are doors that open to anyplace and anything. Those doors are the covers of books!

A   B   C   D
○   ○   ○   ○

A

18. By the time you read this, your Raceway car may be speeding on the Reading Raceway to Step 23!

A   B   C   D
○   ○   ○   ○

B

19. The whole world is at your finger tips. Turn the pages and it will open for you.

A   B   C   D
○   ○   ○   ○

C

20. When you know the ABC code, no one can take it from you . . . no matter how much he may try.

A   B   C   D
○   ○   ○   ○

D

Sentence
Comprehension

Number Correct

Storybook #10 **6**

Story Comprehension

"What would you like to buy today?" asked Mr. Smith.

Ann put her hand up to the box of gum and said, "I want two of these, please."

Then Ann put her hand from box to box and said, "And two of these in this box, and six of those in that box."

Pam put her hand from box to box, "I will take five sticks of this taffy, and three of these chocolate cherries, please."

1. Ann and Pam went to the _____.

   ○ Snack Hut

   ○ Dress Shop

   ○ Candy Shop

   ○ Hot Dog Stand

2. What was the <u>first</u> thing that Pam got?

   ○ taffy

   ○ chocolate cherries

   ○ gum

   ○ candy apple

Go on ➡

Story Comprehension

3. This story is about _____.
   - ○ a trip to the beach
   - ○ shopping for a dress
   - ○ Pam and Ann playing
   - ○ a trip to the Candy Shop

4. Pam asked for _____.
   - ○ gum and taffy
   - ○ taffy and chocolate cherries
   - ○ gum and chocolate cherries
   - ○ mints

5. It seems that Pam and Ann _____.
   - ○ are sad the candy was gone
   - ○ did not like to see Mr. Smith
   - ○ had fun buying candy
   - ○ do not like candy

Go on

Story Comprehension

Look back if you need help.

By the time you read this, your Raceway car may be speeding on the Language Arts Raceway to Step 23! Why are you doing this? So you will be a good reader!

When you know the ABC code, no one can take it from you . . . no matter how much he may try . . . and even if he is sly, it is yours forever!

With the ABC code you can read anything you want. There are doors that open to anyplace and anything. Those doors are the covers of books!

6. What Step will you be on when you read this?

    Step 21   Step 20   Step 32   Step 23
     ○   ○   ○   ○

7. Why are you going on the Language Arts Raceway?

    ○   so you will be a good reader

    ○   to play

    ○   to sing

    ○   to cry

8. You will like to _____ when you know the ABC code.

    play   skate   read   cry
    ○   ○   ○   ○

Go on ➤

Sing, Spell Read & Write

Story Comprehension

Look back if you need help.

9. In the story it said, "The whole world is at your finger tips." This means

   ○ you can use a map.

   ○ you can lift a globe.

   ○ you can read about anyplace in the world.

   ○ you can play.

10. This story is about _____.
    playing   singing   reading   jumping
       ○   ○   ○   ○

Story
Comprehension

Number Correct

Name _____   **Date** _____

Sing, Spell Read & Write ®

A Total Language Arts Curriculum
36 Steps to Independent Reading Ability

Book End Assessment for
Phonetic Storybook Reader 11

Student Assessment Record Summary RACEWAY STEP 24	Number Possible	Number Correct	Percentage of Mastery Score	
Word Recognition	20	_____	x 5 = _____ %	
Word Comprehension	20	_____	x 5 = _____ %	
Sentence Comprehension....................	25	_____	x 4 = _____ %	**Total**
Story Comprehension	10	_____	x 10 = _____ %	**Mastery Score:**
			Sum Of _____ % ÷ 4 = _____ %	

Word Recognition and Word Comprehension

Name _____

1 found round sound	**2** towel town growl	**3** sour out snout	**4** gown clown down	**5** loud cloud sprout
6 crown drown frown	**7** mouth scout about	**8** couch pound ground	**9** shower flower flour	**10** ow ! howl bow
11 how now cow	**12** shout proud brown	**13** owl out bow	**14** towel shower flower	**15** frown round scout
16 couch about loud	**17** mouth how sour	**18** sound cloud clown	**19** snout sprout shout	**20** flour brown ground

Word Recognition ☐

Number Correct

Word Comprehension ☐

Number Correct

Sentence Comprehension

Name _____

1. Bozo put on his huge red nose and bowed to Andy.

A ○ B ○ C ○ D ○

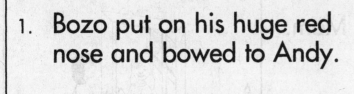

A

2. A clown was in a bath-tub taking a shower.

A ○ B ○ C ○ D ○

B

3. Uncle Howard met Mom and Andy at the big tent.

A ○ B ○ C ○ D ○

C

4. Andy saw a fat clown and a skinny clown.

A ○ B ○ C ○ D ○

D
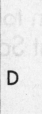

Sentence Comprehension

Name _____

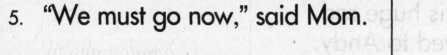

5. "We must go now," said Mom.

   A ○   B ○   C ○   D ○

   A

6. Miss Proud said, "Come in the house."

   A ○   B ○   C ○   D ○

   B

7. Joan gave a loud shout. **"YIPPEE!"**

   A ○   B ○   C ○   D ○

   C

8. Miss Proud then told Mom and Joan about Scouting.

   A ○   B ○   C ○   D ○

   D

   Thank You !

   Good-by.

Sing Spell Read & Write

Sentence Comprehension

Name _____

9. He was looking out the window at the children.

A ○   B ○   C ○   D ○

A

10. Ted, Karen and Liz ran out to make a big snowman.

A ○   B ○   C ○   D ○

B

11. "Look, here is a carrot for his nose," said Ted.

A ○   B ○   C ○   D ○

C

12. Mom put the hat on the snowman.

A ○   B ○   C ○   D ○

D

Sentence Comprehension

RACEWAY STEP **24** ow, ou, ōw ew, qu, wh

13. Bobby and Steve began the raft.

    A ○   B ○   C ○   D ○   E ○

14. It even had a sail on a mast!

    A ○   B ○   C ○   D ○   E ○

15. Bobby and Steve lived near a pond.

    A ○   B ○   C ○   D ○   E ○

16. "Thank you, Mom," said Bobby, and off he flew to meet Steve.

    A ○   B ○   C ○   D ○   E ○

17. "How about a few cookies and some gum to chew?" said Mom.

    A ○   B ○   C ○   D ○   E ○

A

B

C

D

E

Sing Spell Read & Write

Sentence Comprehension

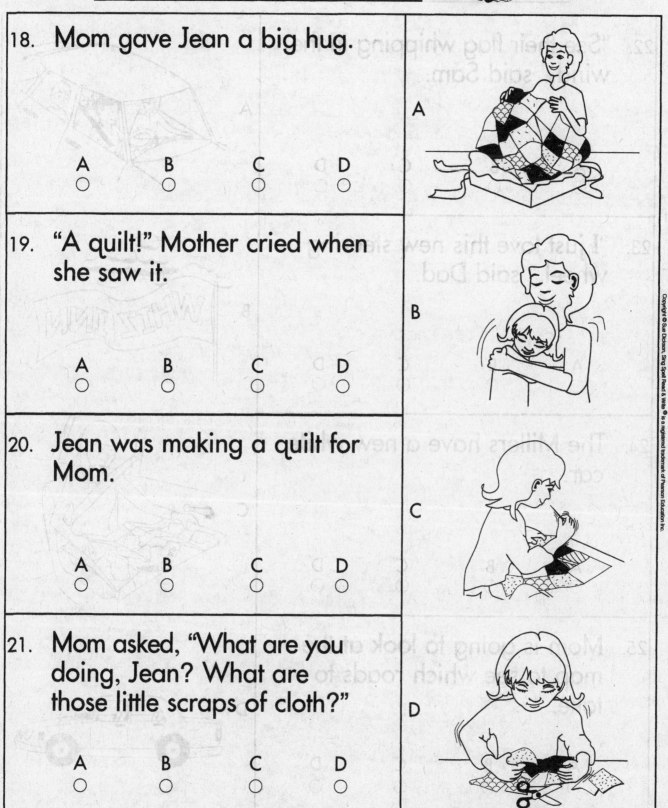

18. Mom gave Jean a big hug.

    A   B   C   D
    ○   ○   ○   ○

19. "A quilt!" Mother cried when she saw it.

    A   B   C   D
    ○   ○   ○   ○

20. Jean was making a quilt for Mom.

    A   B   C   D
    ○   ○   ○   ○

21. Mom asked, "What are you doing, Jean? What are those little scraps of cloth?"

    A   B   C   D
    ○   ○   ○   ○

A

B

C

D

Sentence Comprehension

Name _____

22. "See their flag whipping in the wind," said Sam.

A ○   B ○   C ○   D ○

23. "I just love this new steering wheel," said Dad.

A ○   B ○   C ○   D ○

24. The Millers have a new white car.

A ○   B ○   C ○   D ○

25. Mom is going to look at the map to see which roads to take.

A ○   B ○   C ○   D ○

Sentence Comprehension

Number Correct

7 Storybook #11   Sing Spell Read & Write.

Story Comprehension

Name_____

Uncle Howard and Bozo were pals. "Hi, Andy," said Bozo. "Would you like to see me paint my face?"

"Wow! Yes!" said Andy.

Bozo the Clown put thick white cream on his face.

Then he painted fat red lips.

Next, he put a big red spot on each cheek.

"Now what is missing?" said Bozo with a frown.

"Your big red nose!" said Andy.

Bozo put on his huge red nose and bowed to Andy. Andy just howled!

1. Bozo and _____ were pals.

Uncle Howard   Dad   Mom   Andy
    ○   ○   ○   ○

2. What did Bozo put on <u>first</u>?

○ a big red nose

○ fat red lips

○ a big red spot on each cheek

○ thick white cream

Go on ➡

Story Comprehension

Look back if you need help.

3. What was missing?

   ○ a hat for Bozo

   ○ Uncle Howard's ticket

   ○ Bozo's big red nose

   ○ the can of white cream

4. After Bozo put on his fat red lips he put on _____.

   ○ thick white cream

   ○ a red spot on each cheek

   ○ a big red nose

   ○ a big red hat

5. Did Andy like to see Bozo put on his makeup?

   Yes   No
   ○   ○

Go on ➡

Story Comprehension

Jean was making a quilt for Mom. She would have to quit when Mom's quick steps came near.

"I must get this quilt finished on time," said Jean to herself.

On Mother's birthday, Jean's surprise was finished.

"A quilt!" Mother cried when she saw it. "It is so pretty! This is quite a surprise. Even a queen would love this quilt, Jean!"

"You are my queen, Mom," said Jean.

Mom gave Jean a big hug.

"Thank you, Jean," she said. "I will always see your love in each little stitch of that quilt! Thank you for a very happy birthday!"

6. Jean made a _____.

    doll   book   quilt   cake
    ○   ○   ○   ○

7. She made it for _____.

  ○ her sister's birthday

  ○ her mother's birthday

  ○ her grandmother's birthday

  ○ her teacher's birthday

Go on →

Story Comprehension

Look back if you need help.

8. Why would Jean quit when Mom came near?
   - ○ She was finished.
   - ○ She wanted to surprise Mom.
   - ○ She did not do her job.
   - ○ It was time to stop.

9. How did Mom show she liked the quilt?
   - ○ She sat up.
   - ○ She gave the quilt to Jean.
   - ○ She gave Jean a hug and thanked Jean.
   - ○ She put the quilt in a box.

10. How did Jean make the quilt?
    - ○ She glued it.
    - ○ She stitched it.
    - ○ She cut it.
    - ○ She washed it.

Story
Comprehension

Number Correct

Name _____   Date _____

Sing, Spell Read & Write®

A Total Language Arts Curriculum
36 Steps to Independent Reading Ability

Book End Assessment for
Phonetic Storybook Reader 12

Student Assessment Record Summary RACEWAY STEPS 25	Number Possible	Number Correct	Percentage of Mastery Score
Word Recognition Step 25ᴬ.................	20	_____ x 5 =	_____ %
Word Comprehension Step 25ᴬ...........	20	_____ x 5 =	_____ %
Word Recognition Step 25ᴮ.................	20	_____ x 5 =	_____ %
Word Comprehension Step 25ᴮ...........	20	_____ x 5 =	_____ %
Word Recognition Step 25ᶜ.................	20	_____ x 5 =	_____ %
Word Comprehension Step 25ᶜ...........	20	_____ x 5 =	_____ %
Sentence Comprehension.................	20	_____ x 5 =	_____ %
Story Comprehension	10	_____ x 10 =	_____ %

Total Mastery Score:

Sum Of _____ % ÷ 8 = _____ %

Word Recognition and Word Comprehension

Name _____

1	2	3	4	5
hard	tar	art	shark	star
harm	bar	dart	scar	spark
harp	car	smart	scarf	large

6	7	8	9	10
Mars	arm	target	bark	yard
Carl	jar	garden	park	dark
march	far	party	sharp	yarn

11	12	13	14	15
card	farm	garden	charm	bar
barn	start	park	arm	art
cart	hard	shark	harm	star

16	17	18	19	20
large	yarn	card	march	mark
mark	barn	charm	target	dark
spark	smart	Carl	yard	park

Word Recognition [ ]

Number Correct

Word Comprehension [ ]

Number Correct

Sing Spell Read & Write.

Word Recognition and Word Comprehension

Name _____

1	2	3	4	5
awful	lawn	jaw	August	straw
awning	fawn	saw	applause	Saul
autumn	yawn	paw	because	sauce

6	7	8	9	10
crawl	raw	hawk	automobile	fault
bawl	law	claw	automatic	flaw
Paul	dawn	draw	author	haul

11	12	13	14	15
shawl	saw	dawn	author	haul
sauce	law	fawn	August	bawl
straw	lawn	yawn	autumn	crawl

16	17	18	19	20
awning	awful	claw	fault	raw
applause	automobile	jaw	Paul	paw
automatic	because	hawk	draw	flaw

Word Recognition [ ]

Number Correct

Word Comprehension [ ]

Number Correct

Word Recognition and Word Comprehension

Name _____

1	2	3	4	5
slang	strong	ring	bang	toy
clang	song	king	sang	joy
rang	sing	wing	hang	boy

6	7	8	9	10
enjoy	boil	join	moist	belong
royal	broil	joint	oil	strong
annoy	foil	point	soil	hanger

11	12	13	14	15
bring	Roy	wing	annoy	strong
thing	spoil	hang	broil	rang
along	coin	clang	joint	sang

16	17	18	19	20
join	boy	hanger	soil	thing
coin	Roy	enjoy	foil	sing
soil	oil	royal	joint	king

Word Recognition [   ]
Number Correct

Word Comprehension [   ]
Number Correct

3 Storybook #12   Sing Spell Read & Write.

Sentence Comprehension

Name _____

1. He was lifting hay into a cart.

   A ○   B ○   C ○   D ○   E ○

   A

2. She was dusting her harp.

   A ○   B ○   C ○   D ○   E ○

   B

3. Miss Marcy Sharp sat in the park.

   A ○   B ○   C ○   D ○   E ○

   C

4. Here is an armful of hay for Old Martha.

   A ○   B ○   C ○   D ○   E ○

   D

5. Mark ran to the barn and Sparky ran with him.

   A ○   B ○   C ○   D ○   E ○

   E

Sentence Comprehension

6. He yawned and raised his
   sleepy head.

   A ⃝   B ⃝   C ⃝   D ⃝   E ⃝

   A

7. The mouse was fast and
   jumped in quickly.

   A ⃝   B ⃝   C ⃝   D ⃝   E ⃝

   B

8. He nibbled apples with a
   yawn.

   A ⃝   B ⃝   C ⃝   D ⃝   E ⃝

   C

9. The fawn slowly stamped
   each little paw.

   A ⃝   B ⃝   C ⃝   D ⃝   E ⃝

   D

10. The fawn ran home to tell
    his mother.

    A ⃝   B ⃝   C ⃝   D ⃝   E ⃝

    E

Sing Spell Read & Write.

Sentence Comprehension

Name _____

11. "There is an automatic leaf hose," said Paul.

A ○   B ○   C ○   D ○   E ○

A

12. Saul and Paul are twins.

A ○   B ○   C ○   D ○   E ○

B

13. "Get in the automobile," said Mom.

A ○   B ○   C ○   D ○   E ○

C

LEAF PICK-UP SERVICE

14. Then Saul and Paul fell onto the big pile of autumn leaves.

A ○   B ○   C ○   D ○   E ○

D

Clap!
Clap!

15. You two must get some applause.

A ○   B ○   C ○   D ○   E ○

E

Sentence Comprehension

Name _____

16. Eddy said, "I will be the king."

    A ○ B ○ C ○ D ○ E ○

    A

17. Then he rubbed his wishing ring, and again the gong went **BONG!**

    A ○ B ○ C ○ D ○ E ○

    B

18. Danny grabbed a pipe and had to hang on.

    A ○ B ○ C ○ D ○ E ○

    C

19. She sang a long song.

    A ○ B ○ C ○ D ○ E ○

    D

20. He hung a gong on the top rung of a ladder.

    A ○ B ○ C ○ D ○ E ○

    E

Sentence Comprehension

Number Correct

Story Comprehension

> Saul and Paul are twins. They were seven years old in August. They hardly find fault with each other.
>
> Saul and Paul have a blue wagon. They tied it to their red pedal-car.
>
> "We can help Dad haul the leaves now," said Paul.
>
> "Yes, I like to haul autumn leaves," said Saul.
>
> "This is hard!" said Paul.
>
> Then Saul and Paul fell onto the big pile of autumn leaves.
>
> Such fun it was!

1. Saul and Paul _____ each other.

    like   hate   do not like   kind

    ○   ○   ○   ○

2. The twins were _____.

    ○   ten in August

    ○   seven in April

    ○   six in April

    ○   seven in August

Go on ➡

Story Comprehension

Look back if you need help.

3. The time of the year was _____.

   spring   autumn   summer   winter
   ○   ○   ○   ○

4. What was Paul and Saul's job?
   ○ to haul leaves
   ○ to help Mom
   ○ to play in the leaves
   ○ to shop for a new wagon

5. What was fun for Paul and Saul?
   ○ to fall in the leaves
   ○ to haul the leaves
   ○ to be seven years old
   ○ to go to class

Go on →

Story Comprehension

Look back if you need help.

At our picnic Mom did toil.
In a pot she began to boil
marshmallows,
chocolate,
nuts and cream.
All good things for a happy
Scout's dream.
She didn't let her candy
stew spoil.
She covered it with
aluminum foil.
When more Brownies came
to join,
she gave them each a
chocolate coin.

6. Where were they?
    at camp   at a picnic   in class   at a shop
    ○   ○   ○   ○

7. The boys and girls were _____.

    ○ classmates

    ○ brothers and sisters

    ○ Scouts and Brownies

    ○ teachers

Story Comprehension

Look back if you need help.

8. "At our picnic Mom did toil."
   <u>Toil</u> means
   - ○ played
   - ○ sang
   - ○ worked
   - ○ cried

9. How did the Scouts feel?

   happy ○   sad ○   mad ○   bad ○

10. What did Mom make?

    apples ○   candy ○   a mess ○   dinner ○

Story
Comprehension

Number Correct

Name   Date

Sing, Spell Read & Write ®

A Total Language Arts Curriculum
36 Steps to Independent Reading Ability

Book End Assessment for
Phonetic Storybook Reader 13

Student Assessment Record Summary RACEWAY STEPS 26 - 27	Number Possible	Number Correct	Percentage of Mastery Score	
Word Recognition Step 26ᴀ..................	20	_____	x 5 = _____ %	
Word Comprehension Step 26ᴀ...........	20	_____	x 5 = _____ %	
Word Recognition Step 26ᴮ..................	20	_____	x 5 = _____ %	
Word Comprehension Step 26ᴮ...........	20	_____	x 5 = _____ %	
Word Recognition Step 27ᴀ..................	20	_____	x 5 = _____ %	
Word Comprehension Step 27ᴀ...........	20	_____	x 5 = _____ %	
Word Recognition Step 27ᴮ..................	20	_____	x 5 = _____ %	
Word Comprehension Step 27ᴮ...........	20	_____	x 5 = _____ %	**Total**
Sentence Comprehension....................	25	_____	x 4 = _____ %	**Mastery**
Story Comprehension	10	_____	x10 = _____ %	**Score:**
			Sum Of _____ % ÷ 10 = _____ %	

Word Recognition and Word Comprehension

Name _____

1	2	3	4	5
toot	tool	roof	zoo	broom
boot	pool	loop	too	bloom
root	cool	noon	mood	balloon

6	7	8	9	10
tooth	spoon	shoot	moon	food
smooth	stoop	stool	room	goose
booth	soon	tool	hoop	loose

11	12	13	14	15
poor	noon	boot	balloon	stoop
fool	moon	cool	smooth	hoop
pool	spoon	loop	goose	roof

16	17	18	19	20
fool	food	tooth	broom	booth
stool	root	bloom	zoo	balloon
toot	room	mood	poor	shoot

Word Recognition ⬚

Number Correct

Word Comprehension ⬚

Number Correct

1 Storybook #13

Word Recognition and Word Comprehension

Name _____

1	2	3	4	5
brook	cook	foot	wool	stood
look	good	took	book	shook
hook	hood	wood	crook	hook

6	7	8	9	10
cook	look	brook	wool	good
book	foot	crook	wood	book
took	stood	shook	hood	look

11	12	13	14	15
dictionary	information	foundation	pollution	election
addition	action	information	invention	nation
vacation	station	attention	celebration	addition

16	17	18	19	20
station	information	pollution	action	invention
vacation	invention	foundation	addition	attention
celebration	dictionary	attention	election	vacation

Word Recognition ☐   Word Comprehension ☐

Number Correct   Number Correct

Word Recognition and Word Comprehension

Name _____

1	2	3	4	5
laughter	knight	light	bought	fight
slaughter	bright	slight	thought	tight
ought	fright	might	caught	right

6	7	8	9	10
sought	fought	night	ought	knight
taught	bought	sight	bought	night
naughty	flight	bright	daughter	tight

11	12	13	14	15
thought	fright	slaughter	sight	naughty
taught	caught	slight	light	might
sought	fight	flight	caught	brought

16	17	18	19	20
daughter	night	right	ought	bright
bright	naughty	fight	sight	sought
bought	tight	taught	might	caught

Word Recognition [ ]   Word Comprehension [ ]

Number Correct   Number Correct

3 Storybook #13   Sing Spell Read & Write

Word Recognition and Word Comprehension

Name _____

1	2	3	4	5
eight	sleigh	neighbor	eighty	weight
laugh	trough	rough	cough	enough
dough	sigh	through	though	high

6	7	8	9	10
freight	eighteen	laugh	rough	dough
weigh	neighborhood	tough	enough	eighty
neigh	eightieth	cough	trough	sigh

11	12	13	14	15
tough	neighbor	laugh	high	weigh
high	neighborhood	sleigh	sigh	rough
eight	eightieth	freight	neigh	eighty

16	17	18	19	20
eighteen	dough	weight	eightieth	cough
enough	though	high	tough	rough
neighbor	through	freight	laugh	trough

Word Recognition [   ]

Word Comprehension [   ]

Number Correct

Number Correct

 Storybook #13 **4**

Sentence Comprehension

1. Here is Mother Goose.

   A ○   B ○   C ○   D ○   E ○

2. The polar bears like their pool, too!

   A ○   B ○   C ○   D ○   E ○

3. We can buy our tickets at this booth.

   A ○   B ○   C ○   D ○   E ○

4. He can scoot up to the roof!

   A ○   B ○   C ○   D ○   E ○

5. Their home is a boot!

   A ○   B ○   C ○   D ○   E ○

A

B

C

D

E

Sentence Comprehension

Name _____

---

6. He stood on his left foot.

A ○ B ○ C ○ D ○ E ○

A

---

7. My loose tooth came out!

A ○ B ○ C ○ D ○ E ○

B

---

8. Miss Brooks said, "You may choose whatever you want to do in school."

A ○ B ○ C ○ D ○ E ○

C

---

9. Bill wants to look for a book.

A ○ B ○ C ○ D ○ E ○

D

Look at me! One foot!

---

10. The game has a brook and a pond.

A ○ B ○ C ○ D ○ E ○

E

Choosing Time

Sentence Comprehension

RACEWAY STEPS **26-27** o͝o, o͞o, tion, gh

11. One morning, Mrs. Booth went up to Tom's bedroom.

A ○   B ○   C ○   D ○   E ○

A

12. Tom sat in the booth to eat it.

A ○   B ○   C ○   D ○   E ○

B

13. Tom had to stoop to tie his shoe.

A ○   B ○   C ○   D ○   E ○

C

14. Poor Tom must run!

A ○   B ○   C ○   D ○   E ○

D

15. He sat on a stool to play "Pop the Balloons."

A ○   B ○   C ○   D ○   E ○

E

Sing Spell Read & Write

Sentence Comprehension

Name _____

16. He must take action to stop pollution.

    A ○   B ○   C ○   D ○   E ○

A

17. The U.S. Constitution was a new invention.

    A ○   B ○   C ○   D ○   E ○

B

18. Our leaders speak on TV stations.

    A ○   B ○   C ○   D ○   E ○

C

19. We choose our leaders on Election Day.

    A ○   B ○   C ○   D ○   E ○

D

20. The Fourth of July is the birthday celebration of our nation.

    A ○   B ○   C ○   D ○   E ○

E

Sentence Comprehension

21. Ann was riding in a sleigh through her neighborhood. A B C D E ○ ○ ○ ○ ○	**A**
22. Poor Princess Ann got a terrible fright! A B C D E ○ ○ ○ ○ ○	**B**
23. Her horses neighed and ran back to the palace. A B C D E ○ ○ ○ ○ ○	**C**
24. They bought a house in a pretty neighborhood. A B C D E ○ ○ ○ ○ ○	**D**
25. King Tweek called for a tough knight. A B C D E ○ ○ ○ ○ ○	**E** *The Royal Sleigh*

  Sing Spell Read & Write.

Sentence Comprehension

Number Correct

Story Comprehension

The U.S.A. is our nation.

In the U.S.A. we choose our leaders. We choose them on Election Day. We go to vote.

Our leaders speak on TV stations. They give us information. They tell us about the condition of our nation. They tell us what they will do. They ask us to vote for them.

1. What is the name of our nation?

   U.S.N.   U.S.A.   A.S.U.   S.U.A.
   ○   ○   ○   ○

2. When do we choose our leaders?

   ○   on our birthday

   ○   on New Year's Day

   ○   on Election Day

   ○   on Easter

3. People will vote on Election Day.
   Yes   No
   ○   ○

Go on

Story Comprehension

Look back if you need help.

4. We elect people and they become our _____.

    girls   twins   leaders   nations
      ○   ○   ○   ○

5. Election Day is _____.

    ○ not an important day

    ○ an important day

    ○ a silly day

    ○ a day to play

The laws of the U.S.A. are in a list. The list of laws is called the Constitution.

The U.S. Constitution was a new invention. It was made by the leaders who started our nation.

The laws of the Constitution give us freedom in the U.S.A.

6. What is the list of laws called?

    ○   The List of Laws

    ○   The U.S. Laws

    ○   The invention

    ○   The Constitution

Go on ➡

Story Comprehension

Look back if you need help.

7. Who made the Constitution?

   ○ the leaders who started our nation

   ○ our teacher

   ○ the boys and girls

   ○ our leaders we have now

8. What did the Constitution give us?

   candy   leaders   freedom   inventions
    ○   ○   ○   ○

9. The Constitution is the law of the _____.

   school   U.S.A.   class   town
    ○   ○   ○   ○

10. This story is about _____.

    ○ the leaders

    ○ a teacher

    ○ the Constitution

    ○ boys and girls

Story
Comprehension
Number Correct

Name _____ **Date** _____

Sing, Spell Read & Write ®

A Total Language Arts Curriculum
36 Steps to Independent Reading Ability

Book End Assessment for
Phonetic Storybook Reader 14

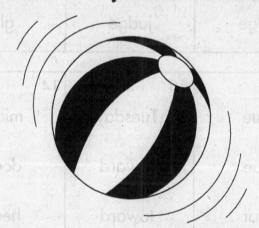

Student Assessment Record Summary RACEWAY STEPS 28 - 29A	Number Possible	Number Correct	Percentage of Mastery Score	
Word Recognition Step 28A..................	20	_____	x 5 = _____ %	
Word Comprehension Step 28A............	20	_____	x 5 = _____ %	
Word Recognition Step 28B..................	20	_____	x 5 = _____ %	
Word Comprehension Step 28B............	20	_____	x 5 = _____ %	
Word Recognition Step 28C..................	20	_____	x 5 = _____ %	
Word Comprehension Step 28C............	20	_____	x 5 = _____ %	
Sentence Comprehension....................	25	_____	x 4 = _____ %	**Total Mastery Score:**
Story Comprehension	10	_____	x 10 = _____ %	
			Sum Of _____ % ÷ 8 = _____ %	

Word Recognition and Word Comprehension*

Name _____

1	2	3	4	5
ball	reward	fudge	true	Tuesday
hall	swarm	dodge	flue	midget
tall	toward	wedge	blue	small

6	7	8	9	10
warm	all	pledge	call	tall
wart	cue	ledge	clue	budge
wall	edge	judge	glue	Sue

11	12	13	14	15
fall	due	Tuesday	midget	fudge
warn	cue	reward	dodge	flue
wedge	war	toward	hedge	fall

16	17	18	19	20
swarm	blue	call	warm	edge
warn	ledge	all	wedge	pledge
true	tall	ball	hedge	glue

Word Recognition [ ]

Number Correct

Word Comprehension [ ]

Number Correct

1 Storybook #14   Sing Spell Read & Write.   *Teacher: Print is size found in some standardized tests.

Word Recognition and Word Comprehension

Name _____

1	2	3	4	5
box	fierce	bear	relax	piece
wax	believe	wear	excuse	relief
tax	priest	great	six	grief

6	7	8	9	10
pear	ax	pier	mix	thief
streak	Max	brief	fox	field
break	ox	shield	fix	tear

11	12	13	14	15
chief	excuse	relax	piece	brief
yield	believe	relief	pear	box
niece	fierce	great	fox	break

16	17	18	19	20
tear	six	steak	grief	yield
tax	mix	field	niece	bear
thief	pier	priest	wear	Max

Word Recognition [   ]

Number Correct

Word Comprehension [   ]

Number Correct

Sing Spell Read & Write   Storybook #14 2

Word Recognition and Word Comprehension

Name _____

1	2	3	4	5
leather	earn	loaf	read	leaves
weather	learn	leaf	deaf	knives
feather	earth	thief	head	wife

6	7	8	9	10
wealth	loaves	bread	pearl	ready
health	knife	thread	heard	steady
breath	leaf	instead	search	heavy

11	12	13	14	15
sweater	thread	learn	heavy	knives
heaven	thieves	leather	heard	wives
dead	thief	loaves	health	wealth

16	17	18	19	20
pearl	read	leaves	breath	heaven
deaf	ready	leather	learn	earth
feather	bread	leaf	knife	weather

Word Recognition ☐ Number Correct

Word Comprehension ☐ Number Correct

3 Storybook #14

Sentence Comprehension

Name _____

1. Mother tied a scarf on her head.

   A ○ B ○ C ○ D ○ E ○

   A
   Wealthy Willie

2. Gus picked up the crab net and stretched to get the crab.

   A ○ B ○ C ○ D ○ E ○

   B

3. Gus had a button. It caught on a nail.

   A ○ B ○ C ○ D ○ E ○

   C

4. A white feather floated down onto Heather's head.

   A ○ B ○ C ○ D ○ E ○

   D
   Will you tell it to me, please Grandpa?

5. "When we finish raking these leaves, I will tell you," said Grandfather.

   A ○ B ○ C ○ D ○ E ○

   E

Sentence Comprehension

Name _____

6. They made a nice warm fire.

A ○   B ○   C ○   D ○   E ○

A

7. Grandmother called from the porch.

A ○   B ○   C ○   D ○   E ○

B

8. She cut the loaf of bread for them.

A ○   B ○   C ○   D ○   E ○

C

9. Tony sat down to relax a bit.

A ○   B ○   C ○   D ○   E ○

D

Grandpa !
Earl !

10. She did not put her name on the valentines, but she gave this clue: 19-21-5.

A ○   B ○   C ○   D ○   E ○

E

Sing Spell Read & Write

Sentence Comprehension

Name _____

11. Ray trimmed the hedge. David cut the grass.

   A ○ B ○ C ○ D ○ E ○

A

12. She wrote: "It is true, I love you" on each one.

   A ○ B ○ C ○ D ○ E ○

B

13. He lifted the latch of the tool shed.

   A ○ B ○ C ○ D ○ E ○

C

14. Ray lifted the tools out of the way.

   A ○ B ○ C ○ D ○ E ○

D

15. Sue started to make her valentines.

   A ○ B ○ C ○ D ○ E ○

E

Sentence Comprehension

Name _____

16. Mrs. Hodges drove over the bridge.

    A ○　B ○　C ○　D ○　E ○

    A

17. Mrs. Hodges gave the boys a big box of fudge.

    A ○　B ○　C ○　D ○　E ○

    B

18. He floated toward a land that's warm.

    A ○　B ○　C ○　D ○　E ○

    C

    Hello, boys !
    What a nice surprise !
    My yard looks wonderful !

19. Safe on the beach the man lay down.

    A ○　B ○　C ○　D ○　E ○

    D

20. Soon little natives swarmed from the town.

    A ○　B ○　C ○　D ○　E ○

    E

7 Storybook #14

Sing Spell Read & Write

Sentence Comprehension

Name _____

21. He sat up with an awful snort!

    A ○ B ○ C ○ D ○ E ○

22. "I will be a pal for you, and I will help in all you do."

    A ○ B ○ C ○ D ○ E ○

23. They waited in the hall to see Coach Dobbs.

    A ○ B ○ C ○ D ○ E ○

24. Soon it was Nick's turn to see the coach.

    A ○ B ○ C ○ D ○ E ○

25. "Thank you, Sir!" Nick said.

    A ○ B ○ C ○ D ○ E ○

Sentence Comprehension

Number Correct

Story Comprehension

The basketball coach was going to pick the team today. All the kids wanted to be on it. They waited in the hall to see Coach Dobbs. Some sat on benches and some leaned on the wall.

The tall kids were sure they would be picked. The not-so-tall kids hoped to be on the team too.

Nick was not-so-tall. He was small, but he played basketball very well. He wished Coach Dobbs would pick him to be on the team.

1. Will all the kids be picked to be on the team?

     Yes   No
     ○   ○

2. Where did the kids wait?

   ○ in a classroom

   ○ in the hall

   ○ at Coach Dobbs' house

   ○ at home

3. Which word does <u>not</u> belong?

   basketball   Coach Dobbs   team   paint
     ○   ○   ○   ○

Go on →

Story Comprehension

Look back if you need help.

4. Who would pick the team?

   ○ the teacher

   ○ the boys and girls

   ○ the moms and dads

   ○ Coach Dobbs

5. Who played basketball very well?

   ○ only the tall kids

   ○ Nick

   ○ Coach Dobbs

   ○ the not-so-tall kids

Uncle Max said, "Tony, do you think you could mix this paint for me? It is thick and lumpy."

Tony was glad to do something by himself. He said, "I am strong. I will try." So Tony started mixing the paint.

After awhile, Uncle Max looked to see if the paint was mixed. "Well," said Uncle Max, "I would say you are as strong as an ox, and as smart as a fox! With such good help, I can be finished before six o'clock!"

Go on

Story Comprehension

Look back if you need help.

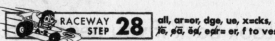

6. Who were working together?

   ○ Tony and Jack

   ○ Uncle Max and Jack

   ○ Tony and Uncle Max

   ○ Jack and Sam

7. Will Tony and Uncle Max be finished today?

   Yes   No
   ○   ○

8. How did Uncle Max feel?

   ○ sad because the paint spilled

   ○ happy because Tony did a good job

   ○ mad because he could not paint

   ○ silly because Tony was stronger

9. Because Tony helped Uncle Max, he finished the job _____.

   quickly   slowly   late   yesterday
   ○   ○   ○   ○

Go on ➡

Sing Spell Read & Write

Story Comprehension

Look back if you need help.

10. Uncle Max said Tony was as strong as an _____ and smart as a _____.

   ○ dog, cat

   ○ ox, fox

   ○ boy, girl

   ○ man, teacher

Story
Comprehension

Number Correct

RACEWAY STEPS **29-30**

ī, u=ōō, air, ui=ōō, or=er
contractions, ār=air,
ā=ō, c=s

Name

Date

Sing, Spell Read & Write ®

A Total Language Arts Curriculum
36 Steps to Independent Reading Ability

Book End Assessment for
Phonetic Storybook Reader 15

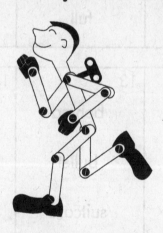

Student Assessment Record Summary RACEWAY STEPS 29 - 30	Number Possible	Number Correct	Percentage of Mastery Score	
Word Recognition Step 29	20	____ x 5 =	_____ %	
Word Comprehension Step 29	20	____ x 5 =	_____ %	
Word Recognition Step 30ᴬ	20	____ x 5 =	_____ %	
Word Comprehension Step 30ᴬ	20	____ x 5 =	_____ %	
Word Recognition Step 30ᴮ	20	____ x 5 =	_____ %	
Word Comprehension Step 30ᴮ	20	____ x 5 =	_____ %	
Sentence Comprehension	20	____ x 5 =	_____ %	**Total Mastery Score:**
Story Comprehension	10	____ x10 =	_____ %	
		Sum Of	_____ % ÷ 8 = _____ %	

Word Recognition and Word Comprehension*

Name _____

1	2	3	4	5
behind	air	put	nuisance	pudding
grind	hair	pull	suitcase	bullet
blind	fair	push	cruise	cushion

6	7	8	9	10
butcher	suit	kind	chair	mind
bush	fruit	find	stair	bind
bull	juice	full	pair	wind

11	12	13	14	15
pudding	put	behind	push	find
nuisance	air	bullet	mind	fruit
butcher	stair	suitcase	bush	fair

16	17	18	19	20
bind	kind	full	cushion	blind
bull	pull	hair	chair	wind
pair	cruise	suit	juice	grind

Word Recognition [   ]

Number Correct

Word Comprehension [   ]

Number Correct

1 Storybook #15   *Teacher: Print is size found in some standardized tests.

Word Recognition and Word Comprehension

Name _____

1	2	3	4	5
worm	don't	favor	mirror	color
worship	didn't	humor	doctor	razor
visitor	can't	flavor	janitor	tractor

6	7	8	9	10
motor	aren't	worry	sailor	author
mayor	we're	world	humor	word
actor	haven't	worth	they're	work

11	12	13	14	15
haven't	visitor	favor	don't	worship
didn't	worth	world	can't	author
we're	doctor	mayor	haven't	actor

16	17	18	19	20
worry	work	world	flavor	worm
janitor	tractor	motor	color	they're
aren't	sailor	mirror	author	razor

Word Recognition [ ]

Number Correct

Word Comprehension [ ]

Number Correct

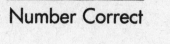

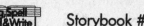 Storybook #15 **2**

Word Recognition and Word Comprehension

Name _____

1	2	3	4	5
bare	circus	wand	police	rare
dare	circle	wash	prince	hare
fare	cent	want	princess	flare

6	7	8	9	10
choice	swamp	spare	groceries	wad
voice	watch	share	concert	wasp
city	watt	care	office	swap

11	12	13	14	15
race	stare	circle	bare	cent
face	father	choice	rare	concert
since	peace	voice	race	flare

16	17	18	19	20
circus	groceries	spare	wash	office
city	wasp	swamp	watt	police
care	dare	swap	since	share

Word Recognition [ ] Word Comprehension [ ]

Number Correct   Number Correct

3 Storybook #15

Sentence Comprehension

Name _____

1. France was having peace after a long war. The Prince of France was happy. He wanted to make his people happy, too.

   A ○ B ○ C ○ D ○ E ○

2. The blind man keeps a dog at his side. The dog helps him find his way.

   A ○ B ○ C ○ D ○ E ○

3. He will teach you to be glad- Not sigh for things you wish you had.

   A ○ B ○ C ○ D ○ E ○

4. It is kind to help the blind cross with the traffic light. The kind do not mind helping the blind.

   A ○ B ○ C ○ D ○ E ○

5. When you see a man who's blind, Do not stay behind him. You will learn from him, you'll find, So, say "hello," and step beside him.

   A ○ B ○ C ○ D ○ E ○

A

B

C
Proclamation of a Celebration for Peace in France

D
I'm tired of my toys. I wish Dad would let me have new ones.
I wish I had a bigger bike.

E

Sentence Comprehension

Name _____

ī, u=ōo, air, ui=ōo, or=er
contractions, ār̄=air,
ä=ō, c=s

---

6. It was a fair day, so Tim went outside to sit in his chair. He took a good book with him.

   A ○   B ○   C ○   D ○   E ○

A

---

7. A squirrel with a bushy tail was on Tim's chair. It ran away when it saw Tim coming.

   A ○   B ○   C ○   D ○   E ○

B

Tim! Come back here and pull the door shut after you!

---

8. People raced to the center of each city. They had no fancy clothes, but they didn't mind. There was cider for all to drink, and dancing for all to enjoy.

   A ○   B ○   C ○   D ○   E ○

C

---

9. Have you ever had a flat tire? We did. We had just paid our fare at the toll booth when . . .
   Bump   bump!   Bump   bump!

   A ○   B ○   C ○   D ○   E ○

D

---

10. When Dad got off the road, Mom said, "Put on your sneakers, Robby. You can't help Dad in bare feet."

    A ○   B ○   C ○   D ○   E ○

E

PAY TOLL

Sing Spell
Read & Write.

Sentence Comprehension

Name _____

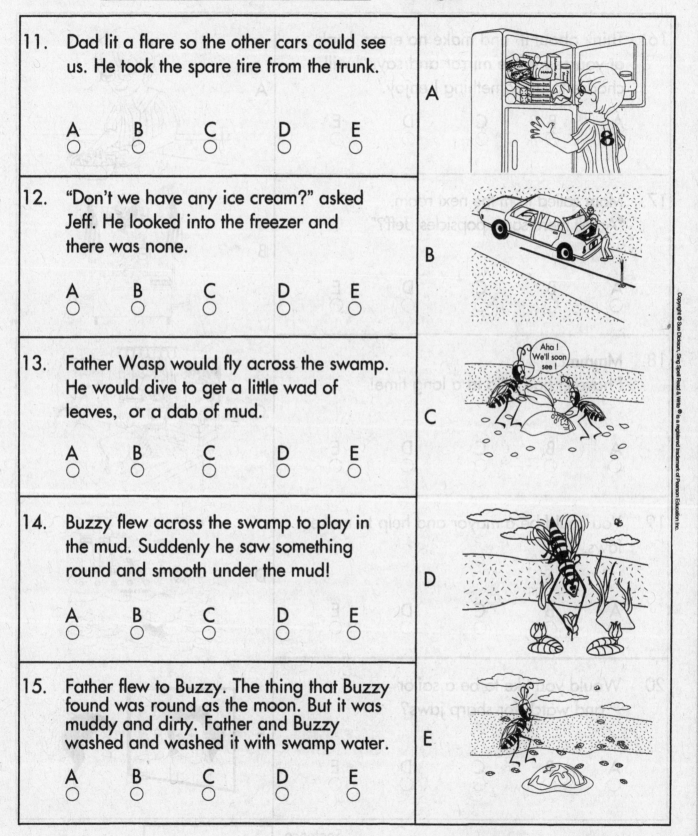

11. Dad lit a flare so the other cars could see us. He took the spare tire from the trunk.

A ○   B ○   C ○   D ○   E ○

12. "Don't we have any ice cream?" asked Jeff. He looked into the freezer and there was none.

A ○   B ○   C ○   D ○   E ○

13. Father Wasp would fly across the swamp. He would dive to get a little wad of leaves, or a dab of mud.

A ○   B ○   C ○   D ○   E ○

14. Buzzy flew across the swamp to play in the mud. Suddenly he saw something round and smooth under the mud!

A ○   B ○   C ○   D ○   E ○

15. Father flew to Buzzy. The thing that Buzzy found was round as the moon. But it was muddy and dirty. Father and Buzzy washed and washed it with swamp water.

A ○   B ○   C ○   D ○   E ○

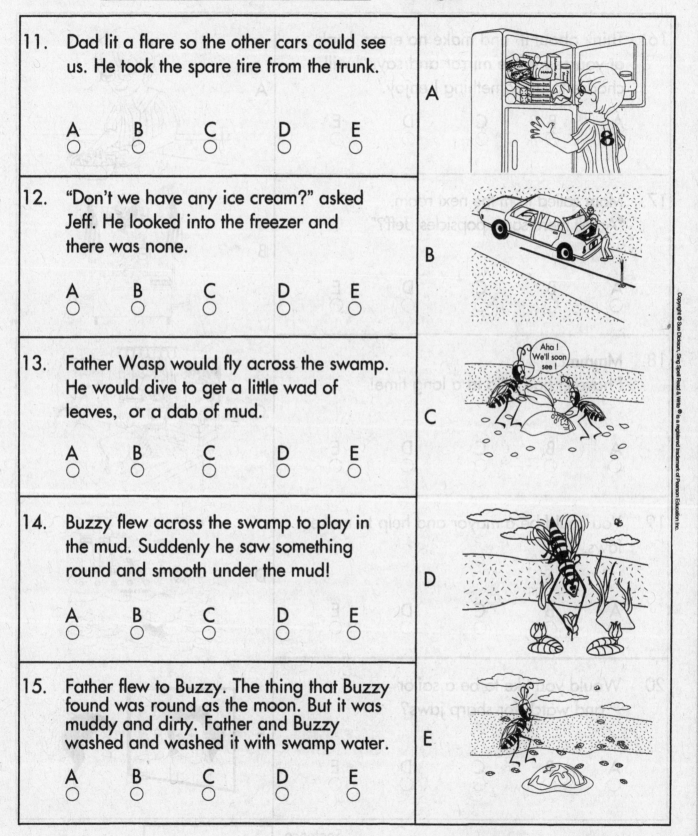

Sentence Comprehension

Name _____

ī, u=ōō, air, ui=ōō, or=er
contractions, ār=air,
ā=ō, ces

16. Think about it, and make no error. Look at yourself in the mirror and say, "I will choose to do something I enjoy."

   A ○   B ○   C ○   D ○   E ○

A

17. Mom called from the next room, "Aren't there some popsicles, Jeff?"

   A ○   B ○   C ○   D ○   E ○

B

18. Mmmm!
   I haven't had jello in a long time!

   A ○   B ○   C ○   D ○   E ○

C

19. You could be a mayor and help to make laws.

   A ○   B ○   C ○   D ○   E ○

D

20. Would you like to be a sailor and watch for sharp jaws?

   A ○   B ○   C ○   D ○   E ○

E

Sentence Comprehension

Number Correct

Story Comprehension

Name _____

RACEWAY STEPS **29-30**

ī, u=ōō, air, ui=ōō, or=er contractions, är=air, ā=ō, c=s

What do you want to be when you grow up?
Do you want to be a mayor?
Or do you want to be an author, a janitor, or an elevator operator?
Think about it and make no error. Look at yourself in the mirror and say, "I will choose to do something I enjoy."
Do your job well and think about this:
It's nice to be important, but it's more important to be nice!

1. This story is about _____.

   ○ going to school

   ○ jobs when you grow up

   ○ a day at the zoo

   ○ time to play

2. Which word does <u>not</u> belong?

   ○ author

   ○ enjoy

   ○ elevator operator

   ○ janitor

3. Pick the job listed <u>in this story</u>.

   King   Teacher   Painter   Author
   ○   ○   ○   ○

Go on

Storybook #15 **8**

Story Comprehension

Look back if you need help.

4. It's more important _____.

   ○ to be pretty

   ○ to be nice

   ○ to be important

   ○ to be silly

5. If you enjoy your job, you will feel _____.

   happy   sad   silly   mad
   ○   ○   ○   ○

Have you ever had a flat tire? We did. We had just paid our fare at the toll booth, when . . .

Bump! Bump! Bump! Bump!

"Oh no!" said Dad.

"Take care," said Mom. "We don't dare stop here. Let's go to the side of the road."

When Dad got off the road, Mom said, "Put on your sneakers, Robby. You can't help Dad in bare feet."

Dad lit a flare so the other cars could see us. He took the spare tire from the trunk.

Dad said I could help. It made me feel good to share the work.

Go on ➡

Story Comprehension

Look back if you need help.

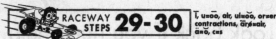

6. When did they get a flat?

   ○ before paying the toll fare

   ○ just after paying the toll fare

   ○ on the highway

   ○ on the driveway at home

7. Where did they stop to fix the tire?

   ○ at the toll booth

   ○ on the road

   ○ at the gas station

   ○ at the side of the road

8. Why did Dad light the flare?

   ○ so the other cars could see them

   ○ so Dad could see in the dark

   ○ because Robby liked flares

   ○ they needed some heat

Go on ➡

Story Comprehension

9. Where did Dad find the spare tire?

    ○ at the gas station

    ○ in the woods

    ○ on the back seat

    ○ in the trunk

10. Do you think Mom, Dad and Robby finished their trip?

    Yes   No
    ○   ○

Story
Comprehension

Number Correct

Name _____   **Date** _____

Sing, Spell Read & Write ®

A Total Language Arts Curriculum
36 Steps to Independent Reading Ability

Book End Assessment for
Phonetic Storybook Reader 16

Student Assessment Record Summary RACEWAY STEPS 31 - 32 - 33	Number Possible	Number Correct	Percentage of Mastery Score	
Word Recognition Step 31	20	_____ x 5 =	_____ %	
Word Comprehension Step 31	20	_____ x 5 =	_____ %	
Word Recognition Step 32	20	_____ x 5 =	_____ %	
Word Comprehension Step 32	20	_____ x 5 =	_____ %	
Word Recognition Step 33	20	_____ x 5 =	_____ %	
Word Comprehension Step 33	20	_____ x 5 =	_____ %	
Sentence Comprehension	20	_____ x 5 =	_____ %	**Total Mastery Score:**
Story Comprehension	10	_____ x 10 =	_____ %	
		Sum Of _____ % ÷ 8 = _____ %		

Word Recognition and Word Comprehension*

Name _____

1	2	3	4	5
write	knot	wreck	knapsack	wrestle
wren	knight	wreath	knowledge	wrench
wrapper	knock	wrinkles	knuckles	written

6	7	8	9	10
knife	answer	knob	toward	know
known	sword	knee	wrote	kneel
knew	wrong	knives	wring	knit

11	12	13	14	15
wrench	wrinkles	wrist	wrench	knot
whole	written	knit	knapsack	wrong
known	knowledge	wrap	wrestle	wreath

16	17	18	19	20
knight	toward	knit	knee	knife
write	answer	wren	wrist	sword
whole	know	knob	knock	wrench

Word Recognition [ ]
Number Correct

Word Comprehension [ ]
Number Correct

1 Storybook #16   *Teacher: Print is size found in some standardized tests.

Word Recognition and Word Comprehension

Name _____

RACEWAY STEP **32** silent *l* silent *b*

1	2	3	4	5
salve	crumb	chalk	doubt	yolk
chalk	numb	salmon	comb	folk
walk	thumb	talk	lamb	calf

6	7	8	9	10
calm	plumber	should	dumb	stalk
half	doubted	would	debt	chalk
palm	climb	could	bomb	comb

11	12	13	14	15
lamb	calm	limb	walk	would
debt	crumb	half	should	doubt
palm	thumb	calf	numb	lamb

16	17	18	19	20
folk	dumb	salve	climb	could
talk	doubted	salmon	debt	comb
stalk	bomb	knowledge	yolk	chalk

Word Recognition [ ] Word Comprehension [ ]

Number Correct   Number Correct   Number Correct

Storybook #16 **2**

Word Recognition and Word Comprehension

Name _____

1	2	3	4	5
sign	fasten	mosquito	glisten	John
resign	listen	antique	bristle	gnat
gnaw	bustle	boutique	gristle	gnash

6	7	8	9	10
honest	castle	croquet	moisten	often
hour	rustle	bouquet	thistle	listen
honor	resign	bustle	whistle	antique

11	12	13	14	15
sign	John	hour	gnat	honest
glisten	rustle	whistle	mosquito	bustle
bristle	croquet	honest	hour	listen

16	17	18	19	20
honor	gnaw	fasten	gnash	hour
thistle	boutique	gristle	bouquet	moisten
often	antique	John	resign	thistle

Word Recognition [ ]

Number Correct

Word Comprehension [ ]

Number Correct

3 Storybook #16

Sentence Comprehension

Name _____

silent
w, k, l, b, g, h, t, qu=k

1. Have you written to Santa?
   If not write today,
   And ask him to put something
   nice in his sleigh.

   A ○ B ○ C ○ D ○ E ○

2. It is time to take all the toys down from the shelves.

   A ○ B ○ C ○ D ○ E ○

3. We will trim all the trees and put trains underneath.

   A ○ B ○ C ○ D ○ E ○

4. Do you want a wristwatch or some tools and a wrench?

   A ○ B ○ C ○ D ○ E ○

5. We will wrap pretty presents.

   A ○ B ○ C ○ D ○ E ○

A

B

C

Dear Santa,
I am writing to tell you
who I am, and where I
live. I hope you will bring
me a truck.

I try to be good, and
to keep my whole room
neat. But it gets messy
fast when I play with my
dog Wrinkles. Please
bring Wrinkles a whole
box of Woofy Dog Chow.

Thank you, Santa
Wil

D

E

Sentence Comprehension

6. The dragon fell on his knees.

    A   B   C   D   E
    ○   ○   ○   ○   ○

A

7. Tom was a brave knight.

    A   B   C   D   E
    ○   ○   ○   ○   ○

B

8. Tom went to find the dragon.

    A   B   C   D   E
    ○   ○   ○   ○   ○

C

9. Tom quickly tied **a big knot** in the dragon's tail.

    A   B   C   D   E
    ○   ○   ○   ○   ○

D

10. Tom took his knife and waved the yellow knit socks.

    A   B   C   D   E
    ○   ○   ○   ○   ○

E

Sing Spell Read & Write.

Sentence Comprehension

Name _____

11. Dad and Sam went fishing.

A ○   B ○   C ○   D ○   E ○

A

12. The itch was on the calf of Sam's leg.

A ○   B ○   C ○   D ○   E ○

B

The Egg Yolk

13. Sam and his folks went for a walk.

A ○   B ○   C ○   D ○   E ○

C

14. Sam fished and fished.

A ○   B ○   C ○   D ○   E ○

D

15. The dining room table must have a bouquet.

A ○   B ○   C ○   D ○   E ○

E

Sentence Comprehension

RACEWAY STEPS **31-32-33**

silent
w, k, l, b, g, h, t, qu=k

16. You must fasten the curtains with new golden chains.

A ○   B ○   C ○   D ○   E ○

17. Moisten those stamps!

A ○   B ○   C ○   D ○   E ○

18. Make King John's bed with his thistledown quilt.

A ○   B ○   C ○   D ○   E ○

19. Hasten to set up a game of croquet.

A ○   B ○   C ○   D ○   E ○

20. Scrub up this castle!

A ○   B ○   C ○   D ○   E ○

A

B

C

Oh, dear! Help!

D

This castle is hard work!

E

Sentence Comprehension

Number Correct

Sing Spell Read & Write.

Story Comprehension

Name _____

Tom was a brave knight. The king knew that Tom was brave.
One day the king called for Tom.

"Could you fight a dragon?" he asked.

"Yes, I know how to fight a dragon," said Tom. "I would hit him and knock him till he fell to his knees."

"Good," said the king. "You must do that."

"I will get ready now," said Tom.

Tom went home to pack a knapsack. In went his big knife. In went his new yellow knit socks. In went his club with the knob on top. In went his book <u>Dragon Knowledge</u>.

1. What was Tom's job?

    ○   He was a king.

    ○   He was a dragon.

    ○   He was a knight.

    ○   He was a teacher.

2. What did the king ask Tom?

    ○   How are you?

    ○   Could you fight a dragon?

    ○   What day is it?

    ○   Are you a brave knight?

Go on ➡

Story Comprehension

3. Could Tom <u>really</u> fight a dragon?

    Yes   No
     ○   ○

4. Did Tom know how to fight a dragon?

    Yes   No
     ○   ○

5. Which word does not belong?

    dragon   knight   king   sock
      ○   ○   ○   ○

6. The <u>first</u> thing Tom put in his knapsack was _____.

   ○   his new yellow knit socks

   ○   his club with the knob on top

   ○   his <u>Dragon Knowledge</u> book

   ○   his big knife

7. <u>After</u> he put in his socks, Tom put in his _____.

   ○   big knife

   ○   club with knob on top

   ○   <u>Dragon Knowledge</u> book

   ○   map of the kingdom

Go on ➡

RACEWAY STEPS **31-32-33** silent

8. What was on top of the club?

   ○ a gem

   ○ a knob

   ○ a nut

   ○ a dragon

9. What was the name of Tom's book?

   ○ <u>A Dragon Tail</u>

   ○ <u>The Dragon Book</u>

   ○ <u>The King and the Knight take a Trip</u>

   ○ <u>Dragon Knowledge</u>

10. This story is about _____.

   ○ the king playing a game

   ○ a knight getting ready to fight a dragon

   ○ The king and the knight take a trip

   ○ the king goes to class

Story
Comprehension

Number Correct

Name _____

Date _____

Sing, Spell Read & Write ®

A Total Language Arts Curriculum
36 Steps to Independent Reading Ability

Book End Assessment for
Phonetic Storybook Reader 17

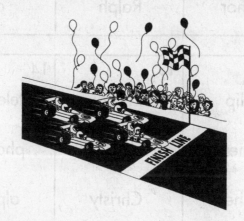

Student Assessment Record Summary RACEWAY STEPS 34 - 35 - 36	Number Possible	Number Correct	Percentage of Mastery Score	
Word Recognition Step 34 - 35ᴬ	20	___ x 5 =	___ %	
Word Comprehension Step 34 -35ᴬ.......	20	___ x 5 =	___ %	
Word Recognition Step 35ᴮ.................	20	___ x 5 =	___ %	
Word Comprehension Step 35ᴮ	20	___ x 5 =	___ %	
Word Recognition Step 36	20	___ x 5 =	___ %	
Word Comprehension Step 36	20	___ x 5 =	___ %	
Sentence Comprehension....................	25	___ x 4 =	___ %	**Total Mastery Score:**
Story Comprehension	10	___ x10 =	___ %	
		Sum Of	___ % ÷ 8 = ___ %	

Word Recognition and Word Comprehension*

Name _____

1	2	3	4	5
phone	charades	mission	Christmas	elephant
phonics	chaise	permission	school	Joseph
photo	parachute	discussion	chorus	dolphin

6	7	8	9	10
Charlotte	Christie	trophy	Chris	photograph
chandelier	chord	orphan	admission	autograph
Chicago	anchor	Ralph	ache	Philadelphia

11	12	13	14	15
stomach	Philip	Christopher	telephone	phonics
Christie	nephew	schedule	pharmacy	Chevrolet
christen	gopher	Christy	alphabet	chandelier

16	17	18	19	20
anchor	Philadelphia	alphabet	discussion	schedule
school	parachute	gopher	permission	Charlotte
stomach	pharmacy	telephone	admission	chord

Word Recognition [   ]   Word Comprehension [   ]

Number Correct   Number Correct

1 Storybook #17   Sing, Spell Read & Write.   *Teacher: Print is size found in some standardized tests.

Word Recognition and Word Comprehension

Name _____

1	2	3	4	5
to	has	your	the	any
of	was	four	easy	very
do	eyes	you	door	built

6	7	8	9	10
two	busy	is	does	said
who	been	as	done	sugar
what	friend	says	soup	shoe

11	12	13	14	15
they	sure	come	was	is
heart	some	one	of	has
love	many	once	said	four

16	17	18	19	20
your	does	to	they	one
who	what	two	the	as
says	very	once	you	do

Word Recognition [ ]   Word Comprehension [ ]

Number Correct   Number Correct

Word Recognition and Word Comprehension

Name _____

1	2	3	4	5
enormous	famous	colonel	curious	Wednesday
explanation	fabulous	pneumonia	serious	garage
subtraction	tomorrow	spaghetti	elevator	sergeant

6	7	8	9	10
dangerous	investigation	gorgeous	pizza	scissors
yesterday	together	generous	ocean	location
department	cafeteria	jealous	vacuum	lieutenant

11	12	13	14	15
colonel	pizza	enormous	yesterday	sergeant
curious	spaghetti	investigation	famous	jealous
gorgeous	elevator	Wednesday	scissors	cafeteria

16	17	18	19	20
dangerous	fabulous	vacuum	garage	ocean
pneumonia	lieutenant	generous	serious	tomorrow
explanation	department	location	subtraction	together

Word Recognition [   ]   Word Comprehension [   ]

Number Correct   Number Correct

Sentence Comprehension

Name _____

1. Brave Heart can make his own shoes. They are very soft shoes. They are made of leather.

   A   B   C   D   E
   ○   ○   ○   ○   ○

A

2. Brave Heart lives near the ocean.

   A   B   C   D   E
   ○   ○   ○   ○   ○

B

3. Brave Heart likes all the animals in the woods.

   A   B   C   D   E
   ○   ○   ○   ○   ○

C

4. It was a maple tree. Sap was dripping from it.

   A   B   C   D   E
   ○   ○   ○   ○   ○

D

5. Once on a Wednesday in early spring two deer came to Brave Heart.

   A   B   C   D   E
   ○   ○   ○   ○   ○

E

Sentence Comprehension

RACEWAY STEPS 34-35-36

ph=f, ch=k, ss=sh, ch=sh, ous
Multisyllable Words,
Rulebreakers & Wacky Words

6. They wrote the alphabet and sang the Phonics Song.

A ○ B ○ C ○ D ○ E ○

A

7. It was a rainy day.
"Phooey!" said Joseph.
"Phooey!" said Ralph.

A ○ B ○ C ○ D ○ E ○

B

8. Ducks and dolphins like rain, but not gophers!

A ○ B ○ C ○ D ○ E ○

C

9. Then the telephone rang.

A ○ B ○ C ○ D ○ E ○

D

10. Ralph put the cassette in the tape player.

A ○ B ○ C ○ D ○ E ○

E

Sing Spell Read & Write

Sentence Comprehension

RACEWAY STEPS **34-35-36**

ph=f, ch=k, ss=sh, ch=sh, ous
Multisyllable Words,
Rulebreakers & Wacky Words

11. What a big Christmas tree was on the Christy Breeze!

A ○   B ○   C ○   D ○   E ○

A

12. I have a stomach ache.

A ○   B ○   C ○   D ○   E ○

B

13. Chris had a good time.

A ○   B ○   C ○   D ○   E ○

C

Merry Christmas from the Christy Breeze

14. Up came the big anchor.

A ○   B ○   C ○   D ○   E ○

D

15. The children made a chorus.

A ○   B ○   C ○   D ○   E ○

E

The Christy Breeze

Sentence Comprehension

Name _____

16. Ed and Sally were sergeants.

A   B   C   D   E
○   ○   ○   ○   ○

17. Tim was the colonel.

A   B   C   D   E
○   ○   ○   ○   ○

18. Ann was the lieutenant.

A   B   C   D   E
○   ○   ○   ○   ○

19. Then they saw some tracks!

A   B   C   D   E
○   ○   ○   ○   ○

20. It is easy if you work together.

A   B   C   D   E
○   ○   ○   ○   ○

A

B

C   Soup anyone?

D

E   There are some **big** tracks here!   Wow! Look   Here's another!   What's up?   They're not mine!

Sing, Spell Read & Write.

Sentence Comprehension

RACEWAY STEPS **34-35-36**

ph=f, ch=k, ss=sh, ch=sh, ous
Multisyllable Words,
Rulebreakers & Wacky Words

21. Bob was curious.

A ○   B ○   C ○   D ○   E ○

22. What an enormous cake!

A ○   B ○   C ○   D ○   E ○

23. Rick was doing subtraction.

A ○   B ○   C ○   D ○   E ○

24. What was going on in the cafeteria?

A ○   B ○   C ○   D ○   E ○

25. Bob took the elevator.

A ○   B ○   C ○   D ○   E ○

Sentence
Comprehension

Number Correct

Storybook #17 **8**

Story Comprehension

Four friends can have fun. They can play together. Tim, Ed, Sally and Ann are friends. They like to play "Secret Spy".

Tim is the biggest. He is going to be the colonel. Ann will be the lieutenant. Ed and Sally are to be sergeants.

Ed and Ann helped build a campsite. Tim and Sally poured soup from the thermos. It is easy if everyone works together.

They went on a hike in the woods. They climbed on some rocks. Then they saw some tracks. After that they played "Secret Spy".

Then they heard many noises! Their hearts began to go "thump, thump!"

"Oh, Rex! You sure did fool us! We are so glad it's you!"

Soon it was time to go home. Tim's dad was at the door.

"Where have you been?" he asked. "Mom has some pizza for your friends hot from the oven!"

1. Mom has just taken the pizza from the stove so it is _____.

   warm   cold   hot   cool
   ○   ○   ○   ○

2. What did the friends like to play?

   ○ Secret Spy

   ○ Tug-of-War

   ○ elevator operator

   ○ janitor

Go on ➡

Story Comprehension

Look back if you need help.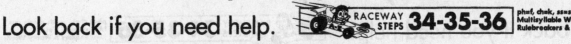

3. Building a campsite and pouring soup was easy because _____ .

   ○ they liked each other

   ○ they worked together

   ○ it was raining

   ○ they did not like each other

4. When did they see the tracks?

   ○ before lunch

   ○ at night

   ○ after they climbed on some rocks

   ○ after they heard some noises

5. Where did the friends go for a hike?

   ○ to the zoo

   ○ to the woods

   ○ to the school

   ○ to the lake

Go on →

Story Comprehension

Look back if you need help. 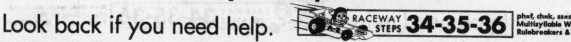 RACEWAY STEPS **34-35-36**

ph=f, ch=k, ss=sh, ch=sh, ous
Multisyllable Words,
Rulebreakers & Wacky Words

6. Why did they go home?

   ○ There was no place else to go.

   ○ It was raining.

   ○ It was time to go.

   ○ It was getting dark.

7. Could this story be true?

   Yes   No
   ○   ○

8. What did Tim and Sally pour soup from?

   ○ a glass

   ○ a pot

   ○ a thermos

   ○ a mug

9. Who was the colonel?

   Ann   Ed   Sally   Tim
   ○   ○   ○   ○

Go on ➡

Story Comprehension

10. A good name for this story is _____.

- ○ "Mom, Dad and the Pizza"

- ○ "Four Friends have Fun"

- ○ "Rex the Dog"

- ○ "Soup for Supper"

Story
Comprehension

Number Correct

Copyright © Sue Dickson. Sing Spell Read & Write ® is a registered trademark of Pearson Education Inc.

Student Record Sheet
for

A Total Language Arts Curriculum
36 Steps to Independent Reading Ability

Achievement Test #1
(To be administered orally)
Raceway Steps 1-15

Student's Name_____ Grade_____ Date_____

Teacher's Name_____ School_____

Examiner's Name_____ Mastery Score _____/%

Total for Section A: _____/24

Total for Section B: _____/20

Total for Section C: _____/20

Total for Section D: _____/36

TOTAL: _____ % of Mastery Score

Student Record Sheet   Achievement #1

SECTION A: Letter Names & Sounds   Raceway Steps 1-3
Have student give the name and sound of each letter. Allow 5 seconds per item. Draw a line through each miscue.

Mm	D	s	o
Hh	R	p	e
Nn	T	w	a
Jj	L	b	u
Ff	V	k	i
Ll	Z	y	a
___/6	___/6	___/6	___/6

Total for SECTION A: ___/24

SECTION B: Blends & Words   Raceway Step 4-14
Have student give the sound of the letter blend. Allow 5 seconds per item. Draw a line through each miscue.

ba	pi	ten	block
be	mo	job	dress
bi	fa	ran	trust
bo	ne	mug	flip
bu	mu	bit	strap
___/5	___/5	___/5	___/5

Total for SECTION B: ___/20

SECTION C: Vocabulary Words from Phonetic Storybook Readers 1-6
Have student read each word. Allow 5 seconds per word. Draw a line through each miscue.

went	camp	as	was
must	grand	the	to
bend	cannot	is	said
stick	flop	a	of
milk	swam	his	have
___/5	___/5	___/5	___/5

Total for SECTION C: ___/20

SECTION D: Sentences from Phonetic Storybook Readers 1-6
Have student read each sentence. Allow 5 seconds per word. Draw a line through each miscue. Subtract the number of miscues from 36 points.

1. A fat cat had ham.
2. Dad can mend the bent pen.
3. Biff has his milk in a tin pan.
4. Todd had a rock and a clock.
5. Gus is snug in the fuzz of his rug.
6. West Camp has a big pond.

Total for SECTION D: ___/36

1 Sing Spell Read & Write

Student Record Sheet
for

A Total Language Arts Curriculum
36 Steps to Independent Reading Ability

Achievement Test #2
Raceway Steps 16-27

Student's Name_____Grade_____Date_____

Teacher's Name_____ School_____

Examiner's Name_____ Mastery Score _____/%

Total for Section A: _____/16

Total for Section B: _____/8

Total for Section C: _____/4

Total for Section D: _____/4

Total for Section E: _____/2

Total for Section F: _____/6

Total for Section G: _____/8

Total for Section H: _____/2

TOTAL: _____ x 2 = ____% of Mastery Score

SECTION A: Letter Cluster Sounds
Have student write the letter cluster for each box. Allow 5 seconds per item. Draw a line through each miscue.

__ __l	__ __bit
sn__ __man	__ __andelier
__ __one	__ __ild
c__ __	b__ __k
m__ __n	__ __m
__ __ell	na __ __ __ __ __
y__ __n	h__ __ __er
t__ __tle	r__ __alty

Sing,Spell Read&Write. Sub-Total for SECTION A: _____/16 STOP

SECTION B: WORD RECOGNITION
Circle the word that names the picture.

1.		moon	spoon
		bus	soil
2.		coat	fox
		little	rock
3.		born	book
		barn	egg
4.		bus	corn
		read	cook
5.		she	chicken
		children	chop
6.		owl	pig
		out	chicken
7.		dish	fish
		shoe	chin
8.		boil	suit
		car	nation

Sub-Total for SECTION B: _____/8

STOP

Sing Spell Read & Write.

2

SECTION C: Word Comprehension

Read the underlined word at the top of each box. Read the four words below it. Circle the word that means almost the same as the underlined word.

1. **shout**	2. **large**	3. **hop**	4. **boat**
yell	slow	sleep	car
wave	pet	jump	bike
ask	fast	listen	ship
laugh	big	climb	clock

STOP

Total for SECTION C: _____/4

SECTION D: Compound Words

Draw lines to match words and make compound words. Remember that compound words are two words put together to make one word.

1. sun   cake
2. cup   boat
3. sail   bow
4. rain   shine

STOP

Total for SECTION D:_____/4

SECTION E: Alphabetical Order

Arrange the two groups of words in A-B-C order by using 1, 2, 3.

goat_____   hay _____

dear_____   want _____

face _____   rest _____

STOP

Total for SECTION E: _____/2

SECTION F: Sentence Comprehension
Look at the four pictures in each box. Read the sentence in the box and put an x on the picture that goes with the sentence.

1. Mark the flowers.

2. Here are two apples.

3. This is a girl.

4. The dog is under the table.

5. What will make you hot?

6. Mark the sign that says you cannot go in.

Total for SECTION F: _____ /6

SECTION G: Rhyming Words

Read the three words in each box. Circle the two words in each box that rhyme.

1. look moon soon	2. log big frog	3. corn horn gain	4. hook like crook
5. less mess this	6. long song sing	7. boy soil boil	8. come love some

STOP

Total for SECTION G: _____/8

SECTION H: Punctuation

Read the sentences and put a period or question mark at the end of each sentence.

1. The girl can curl her hair__

2. Is the little bird hurt__

STOP

Total for SECTION H: _____/2

Student Record Sheet
for

A Total Language Arts Curriculum
36 Steps to Independent Reading Ability

Achievement Test #3
Raceway Steps 28-36

Student's Name_____Grade_____Date_____

Teacher's Name_____ School_____

Examiner's Name_____ Mastery Score _____/%

Total for Section A: _____/12

Total for Section B: _____/6

Total for Section C: _____/6

Total for Section D: _____/10

Total for Section E: _____/8

Total for Section F: _____/8

TOTAL: _____ x 2 = ____%

SECTION A: Spelling
Circle the correct spelling for each word.

1. gloo	glue	glew	7. knee	nee	nei
2. bread	breid	red	8. caf	calf	kafe
3. ofen	often	oftin	9. miet	might	wmite
4. werd	word	wird	10. lamb	lam	lame
5. coler	color	culler	11. haf	half	hafe
6. rong	wrong	runge	12. sign	sine	sien

Total for Section A: _____ /12

SECTION B: Compound Words
Draw a line to divide the compound word into two words.

1. i n s i d e

2. s u i t c a s e

3. o u t d o o r s

4. d o l l h o u s e

5. a f t e r n o o n

6. b i r t h d a y

Total for Section B: _____ /6

SECTION C: Contractions
Write the two words for each contraction.

1. didn't = _____ _____

2. isn't = _____ _____

3. aren't = _____ _____

4. you're = _____ _____

5. hasn't = _____ _____

6. haven't = _____ _____

Total for Section C: _____ /6

SECTION D: Word Recognition
Circle the word that names the picture.

1.	tricycle	circle	
	bicycle	office	
2.	other	mother	
	worm	world	
3.	hear	bear	
	great	steak	
4.	weather	head	
	deaf	feather	
5.	fruit	full	
	suit	wind	
6.	bull	bush	
	chair	hair	
7.	work	word	
	worm	world	
8.	actor	mirror	
	color	tractor	
9.	watch	swap	
	wash	want	
10.	trophy	phone	
	orphan	photo	

STOP

Sub-Total for Section D: _____ /10

SECTION E: Sentence Comprehension
Read the sentences. Put an X on the correct picture.

1. This clown is in the circus.

2. Mom needs eggs. Where could she buy them?

3. Put an X on the animal that lives in water.

4. A girl had $1.00 to spend at the store. What could she buy?

5. This letter has an address on it.

6. Put an X on the shortest tree.

7. The cowboy is resting under a tree.

8. Mrs. Jones had pizza for lunch. Where did she buy it?

Sub-Total for Section E: _____ /8

SECTION F: Story Comprehension
Read the story. Next, read the question and bubble in the correct answer.

John gave his mom a present. It was her special day. The present was a big bunch of pretty flowers. He picked them from the garden. He tied a pink ribbon around the flowers.

1. What kind of boy is John?

   ○ kind
   ○ selfish
   ○ mean

2. Where did John get the flowers?
   ○ store
   ○ garden
   ○ friend

3. What was the last thing John did?
   ○ Give the flowers to Mom.
   ○ Tie the flowers with a ribbon.
   ○ Pick the flowers.

4. How does Mom feel?
   ○ sad
   ○ happy
   ○ mad

5. Why did John give his mom a present?
   ○ It was her birthday.
   ○ Mom was sick.
   ○ It is John's birthday.

6. What did John do first?
   ○ Give the flowers to Mom.
   ○ Tie the flowers with a ribbon.
   ○ Pick the flowers.

7. What color was the ribbon?
   ○ red
   ○ blue
   ○ pink

8. What is a good title for this story?
   ○ "A Bad Day"
   ○ "Mom's Birthday Surprise"
   ○ "The Dragon"

STOP
Sub-Total for Section F: _____ /8

SECTION B: Reading Comprehension
Read the story. Next, read the question and bubble in the correct answer.

John gave his mom a present. It was her special day. The present was a big bunch of pretty flowers. He picked them from the garden. He tied a pink ribbon around the flowers.

1. What kind of boy is John?
   a. king
   b. selfish
   c. mean

2. Where did John get the flowers?
   a. store
   b. garden
   c. friend

3. What did John do first?
   a. Give the flowers to Mom.
   b. Tie the flowers with a ribbon.
   c. Pick the flowers.

4. How does Mom feel?
   a. sad
   b. happy
   c. mad

5. What was the last thing John did?
   a. Give the flowers to Mom.
   b. Tie the flowers with a ribbon.
   c. Pick the flowers.

6. Why did John give his mom a present?
   a. It was her birthday.
   b. Mom was sick.
   c. It is John's birthday

7. What color was the ribbon?
   a. red
   b. blue
   c. pink

8. What is a good title for this story?
   a. "A Bad Day"
   b. "Mom's Birthday Surprise"
   c. "The Dragon"

STOP

Sub-Total for Section B: _____

WINNER

Name: _____

School: _____

Grade : _____

Date : _____

This is to certify that the student named above
has completed the Level 1 Raceway Program
of

Sing,Spell Read&Write®

36 Steps to Independent Reading Ability

Teacher: _____

Principal: _____